YOU CAN DO IT

Things You Can Do To
WITNESS
CHRIST

JOHN WOLLENBURG SIAS

CONCORDIA PUBLISHING HOUSE · SAINT LOUIS

1 2 3 4 5 6 7 8 9 10   22 21 20 19 18 17 16 15 14 13

Introduction   4

1 — Witness Christ Where He Speaks
      and Works   7

2 — Witness Christ as an Expert Witness:
      Law and Gospel   25

3 — Witness Christ as an Expert Witness
      Justification by Faith & the Sacraments   45

4 — Witness Christ in Life
      as Well as Words   62

5 — Witness Christ on the Front Lines   78

      Conclusion   95

The goal of this little book is to help you understand your witness to Christ as an organic part of your entire life of faith in Jesus—and as an organic part of the life of a Christian congregation. Understand *organic* here in the sense of organs working together, largely without needing thought to make them breathe or digest lunch. You don't have to think about your liver, but it lives in harmony with the whole body and performs its various functions. In the same way, the whole life of a Christian bears witness to Jesus without the Christian necessarily thinking, "Time to go and bear witness now!" Paul calls it "This mystery, which is Christ in you" (Colossians 1:27). It is, simply put, living by faith and knowing a little of how to explain what that faith is.

Odds are that you feel the Gospel would be as good for your neighbors as it is for you and you'd like some pointers on sharing it with them. Perhaps you are looking for the courage or the words to broach a topic that, even more than politics, seems taboo. Perhaps you have an idea what to say but wonder where, with whom, and how. Or perhaps you've even given it a shot and wonder why your little pew still isn't full, not to speak of the rest of them!

Though the Bible doesn't have a section titled "How to Witness Christ," the Scriptures certainly care about us bearing witness to the Gospel of Jesus Christ. So also do we Lutherans, who underscore in our Bibles that "the gospel . . . is the power of God for salvation" (Romans 1:16). What we call *witness* is so integral to the Christian faith and life that it can't be separated out into a list of requirements, steps, suggestions, or tips. There are books and programs that attempt to do that, to arm you with three or four questions and muster you out to knock on doors. But the Bible doesn't talk about this sort of program. Indeed, the more we think of sharing the Gospel like selling something, the more advertisement-wearied consumers decide we, too, are simply out to make a buck—or maybe earn eternal rewards—selling them one more thing they don't really need!

Though this book has five simple suggestions that are well within your reach (in some ways, you are probably already doing them), it is not the sort of do-it-yourself book that gets you out "witnessing" in a few easy steps or a few hours of your week. Witnessing is not learning a new skill, such as changing your car's oil or doing brain surgery. Much less is it learning the marketing business and a few good pitches!

Just as the Spirit gives hope and joy and peace, so also He gives us opportunities for witness as we live by faith in Jesus and in love of our neighbor. This book aims to help you "[be] prepared" in those instances "to make a defense to anyone who asks you for a reason for the hope that is in you" (1 Peter 3:15).

Therefore, since we are surrounded by so great a cloud of witnesses, let us also lay aside every weight, and sin which clings so closely, and let us run with endurance the race that is set before us, looking to Jesus, the founder and perfecter of our faith, who for the joy that was set before Him endured the cross, despising the shame, and is seated at the right hand of the throne of God. (Hebrews 12:1–2)

> For we did not follow cleverly devised myths when we made known to you the power and coming of our Lord Jesus Christ, but we were eyewitnesses of His majesty. (2 Peter 1:16)

What does it mean to "witness" or to "be

a witness"? One might witness an accident, witness a marriage, or be a witness for the prosecution or defense. More to the point, one might witness Christ. What does this mean?

The Apostles Witnessed Jesus

To call ourselves "witnesses to Jesus" or to say "I witness to Jesus" is to borrow a term at least thirdhand (or fourthhand, if we count the Lord as the original witness—see John 1:18; 8:14–18; 15:26; 1 John 5:6; Revelation 1:5). From whom are we borrowing this term, and how?

To bear witness *to* something, of course, you have to first witness the thing. The Greek word usually translated as the noun "witness"—*martus*, plural *martures*—originally meant someone who testifies in court, especially referring to what that person has seen or heard. In that sense, it's used several times in Jesus' trial, of all the false witnesses brought against Him. Regarding witnesses for Jesus, He tells His apostles just before He ascends into heaven, "Thus it is written, that the Christ should suffer and on the third day rise from the dead, and that repentance and forgiveness of sins should be proclaimed in His name to all nations, beginning from Jerusalem. You are witnesses of these things" (Luke 24:46–48). Here, again, the word for "witnesses" is *martures*. When Judas Iscariot's vacated seat among the Twelve had to be filled, the qualification was being an eyewitness to Jesus' ministry, death, and resurrection (Acts 1:21–22). Actually, Peter makes this not only the qualification but also the job description of apostles: being *martures* to His resurrection. The Book of Acts chronicles the apostles' witness to Christ (Acts 2:32; 3:15; 4:33; 10:41).

So, when I was asked to write a book on "five steps to witness Christ," I joked that step 1 would be acquiring a time machine and step 2 would be setting it to about AD 30. It would have been a short book but a tall order! We're not witnesses in that way, as replacements for or additions to the apostles. Nor is that necessary, thanks be to God. Rather, "the word is near you" (Romans 10:8), and through it is our witness to Jesus. The apostles handed down the authoritative witness for us in the apostolic Scriptures, guided by the Holy Spirit, to tell once and for all the facts of who Jesus is and what He did and said (John 14:25–26; 15:26–27; 16:12–15; 21:24).

Our faith—and therefore our witness—latches on, not to our feelings or ideas about God or our experiences, but to the fact that Christ has done these things. It attaches especially to the heart of it, that He died on account of our sins and rose on account of our justification (Romans 4:25), and to the truth that by Word and Sacrament, He applies these saving facts to us. "Blessed," Jesus says, "are those who have not seen and yet have believed" (John 20:29). Blessed are we through what is written for us by these apostolic eyewitnesses and what is preached to us from it, so that we are built on their words (Ephesians 2:19–20). Of their good confession, Jesus says, "On this rock I will build My church" (Matthew 16:18). In the second and third chapters, we will explore further that foundation: their confession and ours.

Once these apostles had followed their Lord on to glory (all but John being killed for their testimony to Jesus), the Early Church began to refer to all those murdered for their confession of the faith, all who added the seal of life to the words they spoke, as martyrs, witnesses (Revelation 12:11; 17:6). Stephen is the first (Acts 22:20) to get the term secondhand from the apostles. If, then, the term *witness* comes to us, it is thirdhand from them.

Chapter 4 will unfold how we follow also in the footsteps of the firsthand witnesses, witnessing to Jesus with more than words—with also our lives—as living martyrs. Chapter 5 will look at how our witness faces opposition, just as the apostles surely did. No one should take lightly following in the footsteps of the apostles and martyrs! Our witness to Jesus is something to think about seriously; hence this book. Yet the power of God is made perfect in our weakness, and His grace will be sufficient for us, as it was for them (2 Corinthians 12:9).

Jesus Is Not Gone but Is Alive and with Us

For now, I'd like to begin with how in a certain way you are, with the apostles, a direct witness to the living, speaking, acting Jesus—even without a time machine. "He has risen; He is not here" (Mark 16:6) is not the end of His story. The angels said that of His tomb, not of His Church. Of His Church, Christ says, "Where two or three are gathered in My name, there am I among them" (Matthew 18:20), and, "Behold, I am with you always, to the end of the age" (Matthew 28:20).

Thus, in addition to passing on the apostles' witness to who Jesus is and what He has done, we see by faith that He is still speaking and working among us. That's not simply in a nebulous way, like an imaginary friend, a cozy feeling, or the experience that things seem to be working out better for us with Him than we suspect they would if we were on our own. You hear a lot of God talk like that, but it's not a full or accurate picture of Jesus, and that is what matters for our witness! "For this is the will of My Father, that everyone who looks on the Son and believes in Him should have eternal life, and I will raise him up," our Lord says, "on the last day" (John 6:40).

We have definite promises of ways that Jesus is with us to speak and act. He said first to His apostles and now to pastors, "As the Father has sent Me, even so I am sending you. . . . If you forgive the sins of any, they are forgiven them; if you withhold forgiveness from any, it is withheld" (John 20:21, 23); "The one who hears you hears Me" (Luke 10:16);

and even, "Take, eat; this is My body. . . . Drink of it, all of you, for this is My blood" (Matthew 26:26–28).

You are witnesses of these things. Jesus is not done speaking and acting (Acts 1:1–8) but promises still to do so by the Spirit through those He sends. God's Word spoken by these pastors in His stead and by His command "is just as valid and certain, even in heaven, as if Christ our dear Lord dealt with us Himself" (Small Catechism, Confession). That is truly something to see, or rather hear, and bear witness to!

Therefore, the first step of being a witness to Jesus is being where He has promised to and does speak and act—and being attuned to what He is saying and doing. As Luther says, "We should fear and love God so that we do not despise preaching and His Word, but hold it sacred and gladly hear and learn it" (Small Catechism, Third Commandment). That is our earthly Sabbath rest in Jesus, and we ought not despise it—not only for our sake, but also for the sake of our neighbors, friends, and families. Witnessing to others starts with receiving what Jesus is doing for us in the Divine Service. We, like the Samaritan woman at the well (John 4:1–42), should want to tell others what He is doing for us so they can come and have Him do it for them. Perhaps, like her townsfolk, the people we tell will then say, "It is no longer because of what you said that we believe, for we have heard for ourselves, and we know that this is indeed the Savior of the world" (John 4:42). If this is what we want, then we ought to know and be able to explain what it is that He is doing among us!

You Witness Jesus Where He Comes to You

I said at the outset that you are almost certainly already doing, to some extent, things that bear witness to Jesus, because the whole Christian life is to do that (Matthew 5:13–16; Ephesians 4:1–6). The first of those things is pretty obvious: you give a witness simply by "not neglecting to meet together, as is the habit of some" (Hebrews 10:25). By putting your rear in a pew when the Word of God is preached and the Lord's Supper administered, instead of sleeping or working or playing—like most of your neighbors—you are saying with Peter, "Lord, to whom shall we go? You have the words of eternal life" (John 6:68). That's a witness in itself. It's clearest to those to whom God has given you a special opportunity and responsibility to be a witness: your family (whether of blood or of faith) and your closest neighbors and friends, who know where you are and what you do.

To put it bluntly the other way: if you are not faithful in attending your Lord when He comes, why should anyone else listen to you when you speak about Him? Why should they think they should be where you often are not?

Of course, simply being marked present doesn't exhaust your witness, your testimony, in the Divine Service. What witness does it give to your fellow Christians or to visitors if you appear to be aiming merely for attendance? Do you listen attentively to the readings from God's Word and the sermon and help your children learn to do the same? Do you treat the words coming from the pastor as words coming from God's servant and meant by God for your salvation? When the liturgy bids you respond with "Amen"—"Yes, yes, it shall be so," as Luther puts it (Small Catechism, Conclusion to the Lord's Prayer)—do you say it with vigor and certainty? Or might that word at the end of your prayers just as well be a shrugged "whatever"?

Likewise, how do you respond when you are invited to sing with "angels and archangels and all the company of heaven," the joyful song of the heavenly throne room, "Holy, Holy, Holy" (see *LSB*, p. 161)? Joined to the angels' song is the song at Jerusalem's yearning gates, "Hosanna," where Christ Himself comes to you in the flesh by humble means to enliven soul and heart and body with the foretaste of the feast to come. Thus we sing, preparing to eat the holiest and most precious food on earth: the body and blood of the Son of God, given into death to save you from all sin, death, and the power of the devil. Quite a song befits that occasion—"as often as you eat this bread and drink the cup"—so as to "proclaim the Lord's death until He comes" (1 Corinthians 11:26). Such a song teaches (Colossians 3:15–17)! What is more full of awe and more full of joy? Maybe you've never thought that way about the Sanctus, sung before the Words of Institution in the Lord's Supper. Do these words have your attention? Your fullness of voice and heart? Do you plumb these inspired words, meaningfully combined, like a gold mine for the treasures packed into them?

Lutherans are often accused of a stodgy service, full of dead formalities. Perhaps that is because those unfamiliar with it don't understand it. Or perhaps we ourselves act as if it were either unfamiliar or so empty of substance as to be worn out by too much familiarity. That would be a sad witness indeed, if we act as if our Lord's coming to us is ho-hum!

Don't get me wrong; you don't have to possess the voice of an angel and the lungs of a diva. While the Lutheran Church has been called the singing church, we don't have auditions. I'm a tenor but not one of the three great ones, not by a long shot! Here's the point: the character of our worship in the texts we use, how we use them, and our full participation in them should reflect in fullest measure what is happening here where our Lord Himself comes down to save us. That is what the Divine Service is all about!

The pastor does not carry that responsibility alone, though he has the leading part. You have a witness to give there too, to hear the Word of Jesus as the Word that saves you and leads you into all truth and to join your voice with the rest of the faithful, even the angels and archangels and all the company of heaven. This is a high and holy privilege. Don't let it look and sound like something of little consequence. Good things take effort, and there is a witness given, good or bad. Let it be a good one!

Such self-examination might go beyond what you expected in a witnessing book, but since witness is and must be more than skin deep, sometimes we might poke where it hurts! Hopefully, that's not entirely unfamiliar. We live as saints and sinners, at the same time suffering the condemnation of the Law—even and especially on our best efforts—and being comforted in the Gospel, the certainty that where we have been unfaithful, Christ is faithful and forgives our sins.

He establishes our identity before God, not in our failings, which are many, but in His perfection, which is complete. In that, in the blood of Jesus for us, and in His righteousness—and not in thinking we've done as much as could reasonably be asked—is our joy, our hope, and our unfailing great reward. This treasure buried in daily repentance and the forgiveness of sins is the aim of everything Christ's Church does and is (Large Catechism II 55). So repent, believe the Gospel, rejoice, and bear witness!

What about Those Visitors?

It's sometimes observed that visitors to a Lutheran church feel less immediately at home than in other churches because of our liturgical service. Although totally familiar to the whole Church (not just Lutherans) of ages past, it is today unfamiliar or uncomfortable to some. The liturgy has peculiar and weighty words. It assumes that those participating have been taught what those words mean and what the liturgy is doing. That doesn't mean that the liturgy's time has passed—far from it—but that we (pastors and people) ought to be prepared to help the unfamiliar understand what is going on!

Couldn't it be simplified and made comfortable for the family off the street? Not so easily if the Divine Service is to keep giving what Christ intends it to give: not just milk but spiritual meat for those who are there Sunday to Sunday, year to year, Baptism to funeral. What the service is doing for them is weighty and important, a matter of eternal life and death.

Think about a doctor's office. When you go there, it's not a totally comfortable experience. He talks about things you'd rather not think about. He uses technical words you wouldn't use otherwise. He might give you a frightening diagnosis, and you might not understand everything all at once, but you are there to get the right treatment. You don't want to make yourself at home there and have the doctor chuckle and offer platitudes. You want to be healed, even if it is uncomfortable at first. That's what the doctor is for. How much more so the Divine Service, where the deadly disease of sin is diagnosed and the medicine of immortality dispensed!

Or think about a football game. I watch football with Heidi, my wife, but she's the real fan. Oh, I know the basic rules, positions, and plays, but anyone could tell that we enjoy the game on different levels. To me, much of it is noise, and the game would take forever if the referees had to explain the particulars of every penalty so I would know exactly what was going on. A certain amount of specialized knowledge is needed to get the most out of it. Perhaps you're a devoted football or basketball or golf fan. Are you a devoted fan of the Divine Service, interested enough to invest some effort and figure out what's going on? If not, why not?

I mention these examples to encourage you to learn more about what we do in the Divine Service and why we do it—both for your sake, so your faith will latch on to these handholds put there for it, as well as for the sake of your witness to others. Your pastor can help you.

Imagine a visitor sitting near you in church. What help might he or she appreciate in navigating the service and hymns? Imagine how you could help answer questions or explain what he or she has stumbled into here, that it is not dead ritual or empty formalism, but Christ Jesus visiting His people to forgive their sins. That would be a personal witness that shows how greatly you value and benefit from what is going on here.

A great book to begin your exploration and further your understanding of the Divine Service is CPH's *Worshiping with Angels and Archangels.*

So, Why Are You There?

Giving such a good witness to others in the Divine Service calls for us to think about why we are there—not a bad thing to consider anyway! Why you go to church is likely a mystery to your absent friends and neighbors, and maybe also to your children, siblings, or even parents. That's worth thinking about, for understanding how to witness to them. Most people assume, I think, that it is out of obligation—and that it's one obligation they'd rather avoid if they can!

If they've thought about it, they might think that the hour or so of your Sunday morning, or whenever, is time you think you owe to your God, a tax of thankfulness on the seven days a week He gives you. If they were to diagram your week for you, Sunday afternoon through Saturday would be a big down arrow of blessings from your God to you, and Sunday morning would be an arrow going back up from you to your God, a sacrifice of sorts. They might even connect the arrows in this way: that you put your time in on Sunday, and presumably some money in the plate, because you figure a little more going up means a lot more coming down. If you do get anything out of that time on Sunday, besides giving up time and praise and offerings, it would be maybe some enjoyment, camaraderie, or advice on how better to do your part the rest of the week and earn an even better reward.

Is that our reality? If so, we need a reality check, for that is not what we believe, teach, or confess. Luther explains that all those good gifts coming down from above are "only out of fatherly, divine goodness and mercy, without any merit or worthiness in me" (Small Catechism, First Article)—not even because we have seen fit to worship Him! As Jesus says, His Father "makes His sun rise on the evil and on the good, and sends rain on the just and on the unjust" (Matthew 5:45). All that is by grace, because God is good and the giver of all good things, not because one person deserves it more than another or is more thankful than the another.

Why, then, if it's all by grace, do you go to church at all? Perhaps because you feel guilty if you don't? God has, after all, commanded us to gather in His name, to hear His Word and eat His Sacrament, to sing His praises, to pray, and to support His Church. It would be rather rude to accept all these blessings and not return thanks.

But command and thankfulness aren't the half of it. Better is the fact that the greatest of all God's gifts and the one on which all else relies—the reason that God upholds the world and sends sun and rain on good and evil alike—is the forgiveness of sins in Christ Jesus our Lord. It is His will that this forgiveness be preached and administered to all people by His definite promises, which are delivered to us chiefly in the Divine Service. We come as often as we can, because while we have His word that we are saints, we still feel the truth in our bones that we are sinners. The truth is, you don't have to go; you get to go!

We come to be washed, forgiven, renewed, fed, and restored as God's people in the assurance that what Jesus has said is true. We believe Him despite the sins that cling to us, the pains that afflict our flesh, and the turmoil in this world of sin. We believe that He is our Lord, that He has redeemed us, that nothing will separate us from His love, and that His grace will be sufficient and will bring us home. That, dear friends, is the Gospel: that His blood covers you; that your death, He has died; that your sins, He has taken upon Himself; and that your life He has assured in His own body and blood, risen and ascended and coming to nourish and sustain you. That is the Gospel, of which Christ's people can never have too much. They hear the voice of their Good Shepherd and come to be fed. How's that for a reason—the reason—you are there Sunday morning?

At the Divine Service, the Lord serves us. That is the motivation of our witness. We are not out to win people to praise God because His ego needs stroking or to augment our dollars with theirs in the offering plate. No, we are witnesses to His powerful working in Word and Sacrament! By these our Lord has ransomed us out of death to real life, and we would share that life. As those reconciled to God, we become reconcilers to God (2 Corinthians 5:14–21), passing on the gift, welcoming the wayward back, and sending abroad the Word that brought us in. We do this because Jesus is the propitiation "not for [our sins] only but also for the sins of the whole world" (1 John 2:2). We do this because it is the will of our loving God, who has brought us to rejoice and participate in His loving will for "all people to be saved and to come to the knowledge of the truth" (1 Timothy 2:4). If not for your own sake, then for the sake of that witness, learn what the Lord is doing for you in the Divine Service, and think about how to explain why you go. Your neighbors (who likely think you go because you have to) might be very surprised!

Key Points

- The apostles are *the* witnesses to Jesus in the truest sense. Our witness (that is, our confession) depends entirely on and must be consistent with theirs.

- The Early Church extended the term *witness* or *martyr* to those who died for their confession of the apostolic faith.

- Our attendance and joyful participation in the Divine Service witness to unbelievers and the lapsed that Jesus is speaking and acting there in the Gospel for the forgiveness of sins.

- For the sake of ourselves and those to whom we might witness, we should appreciate the Divine Service as the place where faith receives the gifts of Christ necessary for our witness.

Discussion Questions

1. How does the Bible use the term *witness*? How did the Early Church adapt it? How does this put our "witnessing Christ" in perspective?

2. A good witness distinguishes between fact and opinion or feeling and is careful to tell not merely truths but the whole truth and nothing but the truth. We all have ways of softening truth into opinion, usually to be polite. You might say, "*I don't think* that bolt unscrews that direction" instead of "Righty-tighty, lefty-loosey." What—perhaps unintentional—misunderstanding do we invite when we bear witness to Jesus this way (that is, saying, "As I see it . . . ," "I believe . . . ," or "I think . . .")? How can we avoid that misunderstanding, while still speaking "with gentleness and respect" (1 Peter 3:15)?

3. Evaluating our witness brings us face-to-face with Law and Gospel, critical words of God that shape the

Christian life. What does the Law say? What does the Gospel say? Which one establishes who we are before God, and why is that important?

4. Where and how are Law and Gospel functioning in your week? How could you see to their working more often or more effectively for you and those close to you?

5. How do the lectionary selections of the Church Year prepare you to be a witness? What gets rehearsed every year? What purpose does repetition serve?

6. This chapter expounded on the Amen and the Sanctus. Browsing a hymnal, pick one or two other pieces of the service or a hymn your congregation used last Sunday and mine it for meaning! What are we witnessing by these words? Why are they good to have in our common vocabulary?

7. If you were called as a witness to a car wreck or a bank robbery, you'd be expected to recount in an understandable way the significant things that happened. Suppose a friend asked you Monday morning, "So, what happened at church?" What would be your witness? What would you assume your friend knew or didn't need to know? What would you definitely make clear?

Action Items

1. **Become a fan of the Divine Service:** Read through the order of the Divine Service your congregation is

using. If it is from *Lutheran Service Book*, look up the Bible references for the various parts. Think about what each part means and how it helps to deliver the goods of Jesus, the forgiveness of sins, and God's promises to you in His Son.

2. Again, thinking on the Divine Service, **consider how you would explain to a guest or family member why we do what we do.** Ask your pastor for insight or resources so you can be prepared. (Maybe he could be persuaded to do a class so everyone could benefit!) Pretend that an unchurched friend or a friend who quit going to church some time ago asked to go with you on a Sunday. How might you prepare them to understand and benefit from the service—and perhaps come back?

3. **Look into how your congregation helps visitors** who attend the Divine Service figure out what is going on and if there is someone knowledgeable to answer their questions if it is unfamiliar. Is your congregation small enough that your pastor can easily do this, or could he use some help from elders or ushers? Do you have information available about the Divine Service and our distinctive Lutheran theology of worship? If not, providing that could improve your congregation's witness to visitors.

4. **Brush up on the theology of worship with the Book of Hebrews:** Read the following, thinking on what

parts of the service they reflect and developing a new appreciation for what you (not *have* to but) *get* to do in the Divine Service: Hebrews 1:1–2; 2:6–9; 4:9–16; 9:11–22; 10:19–25; 12:1–3, 18–24; 13:7–17, 20–21. Think about how to use what you find in your witness to what's going on in the Divine Service.

And I, when I came to you, brothers, did not come proclaiming to you the testimony of God with lofty speech or wisdom. For I decided to know nothing among you except Jesus Christ and Him crucified. (1 Corinthians 2:1–2)

Bearing a witness implies having facts.

Opinions don't count, nor do ideas. "Just the facts, ma'am!" Suppose you testified in court, "The defendant's a great guy—well, at least he's been nice to me." It might be "the truth, the whole truth, and nothing but the truth" about your feelings, but what difference should it make to the jury? On the other hand, if you testified as an expert to the most important facts, "The glove does not fit," "The DNA says otherwise," or "The tomb is empty, and I can show you from the seal and linens why it is so," your testimony could have verdict-changing value—and it should!

Christians often think of a personal testimony as being about the difference you feel Jesus has made in your life: Your family is happier. Your life has more meaning. You feel better about yourself, and He has helped you kick some habit you thought you'd never be rid of. You used to be a (fill in the blank), but now you are (something a lot more socially acceptable). But does this really convey Jesus and His Gospel? Can it actually save anyone?

Jesus' Secret in the Gospel of Mark

In Mark's Gospel, Jesus works many miracles, and often they are followed by a surprise. He cleansed a leper but told him, "See that you say nothing to anyone" (Mark 1:44). He raised Jairus's daughter from the dead but "strictly charged them that no one should know this" (5:43)—likewise, when He restored a deaf-mute's hearing and speech (7:36), and so on. These sound like great personal testimonies; surely He met felt needs, and others could have related. So why didn't He ever say but once, "Go and tell what great things God has done for you"?

The one exception is a man possessed by an unclean spirit. The locals had tried and failed to chain him up; he cried out among the tombs and on mountains and struck himself with stones. The demon, it seems, threw the man at Jesus' feet and spoke through him: "What have You to do with me, Jesus, Son of the Most High God? I adjure You by God, do not torment me" (Mark 5:7).

It seems he didn't even know, or at least couldn't say, what his own problem was: a demon was running the show. So much for felt needs! But Jesus knew and had great mercy on the poor guy. Jesus cast the demon out—actually a whole legion of them. He let them enter some two thousand pigs, which they immediately hurled into the sea. Frightened and angry neighbors then gave Jesus the bum's rush out of town.

The formerly possessed man would gladly have gone with Him, but Jesus said, " 'Go home to your friends and tell them how much the Lord has done for you, and how He has had mercy on you.' And he went away and began to proclaim in the Decapolis how much Jesus had done for him, and everyone marveled" (Mark 5:19–20). That's the one time in Mark where Jesus says—it seems, most improbably—"Go and tell."

Why? Because what Jesus does for this man is closer to the heart of the matter than all the other "hush-hush" miracles. This account of the demon-possessed man is awfully close to Paul's words: "He has delivered us from the domain of darkness and transferred us to the kingdom of His beloved Son, in whom we have redemption, the forgiveness of sins" (Colossians 1:13–14). It echoes Luther's nutshell Gospel: "I believe that Jesus Christ . . . is my Lord, who has redeemed me, a lost and condemned person, purchased and won me from all sins, from death, and from the power of the devil" (Small Catechism, Second Article). That is a good, accurate, and useful witness!

Now that the Gospels are finished, the real, essential point of all true witness is Christ crucified for our sins and raised for our justification (Romans 4:24–25). As little as the world might be looking for that, as little as it wants to identify and feel that need, this good news is "the power of God and the wisdom of God" to save (1 Corinthians 1:24; see also vv. 18–25). That's the point we need to get to if we are to bear witness to the real Jesus. Perhaps this extended introduction from the Gospel of Mark demonstrates how to help a friend with a Bible to see Jesus for who He is. But let's consider a more direct and easier to remember approach by returning to visit an old friend.

Hello, My Old Friend, Mr. Catechism

The aim of this chapter and the next is to help you sharpen your witness to Jesus—your confession of the faith—so that it can be as accurate, to-the-point, and full of the substance of the Word, through which the Holy Spirit works faith, as it can be. Priscilla and Aquila helped Apollos this way (Acts 18:24–28), taking him aside and teaching him "the way of God more accurately" (v. 26). You have a pastor to serve you that way, and I encourage you to make the most of him!

I also imagine that you have an old friend around the house somewhere, Luther's Small Catechism. This little book is a convenient condensed version of the faith, small enough to fit comfortably into the memory and to serve in bite-size pieces for daily devotions. At the same time, it's rich enough to give a solid foundation in the faith—both for you and for those to whom you might speak the word of hope. It shares a fantastic outline of concise and accurate answers to questions about "the hope that is in [us]" (1 Peter 3:15). Here we'll look at the first two parts, the Ten Commandments and the Apostles' Creed, that is, Law and Gospel. The tension between these two fundamental messages—Law and Gospel—in God's Word is crucial to the faith and certainly an aid to our witness.

If you don't have a copy of the Small Catechism, your pastor would gladly help you find one, or you can access one online at bookofconcord.org/smallcatechism.php.

The Law: The Ten Commandments

Though now an endangered species in public places, the Ten Commandments are still probably the most familiar part of the Catechism. But we mustn't assume when we speak our witness that everyone knows what God really means by them.

The Commandments sum up God's will for our relationships to Him (1–3) and to one another (4–10). To be more concise, as Jesus was, "Love the Lord your God with all your heart and with all your soul and with all your mind," and, "Love your neighbor as yourself" (Matthew 22:37, 39). Yet we do well to unpack the Ten Commandments (and Luther's helpful explanations), because we often forget what love looks like and what it does and does not do. Jesus does likewise in His Sermon on the Mount (Matthew 5–7), making clear that the Commandments are meant to strike not only hand and mouth but also eye, ear, and heart, and to strike all people all the time.

To a great extent, the Law is written on the human heart, though the corruption of our nature dulls and twists it. Everyone knows it is wrong to murder or steal. In our day (as in any), the corrosive "futile thinking" of fallen man attacks this natural law (Romans 1:18–32), even in matters of word and deed. Christian citizens, out of love for their neighbors and concern that the government would indeed protect the good and punish the evil as it ought (Romans 13:3–4), have had to speak volumes about the Law to the many working on forgetting it, about abortion and euthanasia, pornography and promiscuity, divorce and homosexuality, greed and aimless violence . . . the list goes on. We have no choice but to come to the aid of a suicidal society by speaking the truth. At the same time, the Law of God does not exist solely to make those outside the Church "straighten up and fly right." And we Lutherans know that! But do they? Not generally. Hence, ears tend to close when they sense the holier-than-thou bit coming on.

As people who like to think of ourselves as lawful, we have the natural impression that laws are meant to be kept and that if a law is given, if we try hard enough, we can keep it. This is a good standard for human laws, as you can't lock up everyone. Our consciences also function this way, as "conflicting thoughts accuse or even excuse" us (Romans 2:15). We assume this is how God's Law works too. And I, naturally, want what I want to be excused as much as possible!

The Law Always Accuses

However, the Law of God never excuses us but always accuses, and when it accuses, there are no petty offenses (Apology of the Augsburg Confession IV 38). The sentence is death. Jesus demands all: heart, soul, mind, and that you should love your neighbor not only just as you would desire to be loved, but even more, as you have been loved by God Himself. Holy is holy. Less holy is not holy at all. There is no such thing as "more sanctified" or "holier" (as in holier-than-thou). God is holy; no one else need apply. He does not say, "Be holier," but "You therefore must be perfect, as your heavenly Father is perfect" (Matthew 5:48).

Luther underscores this in the Ten Commandments by tying the second through tenth explanations by their common introduction, "We should fear and love God so that . . . ," back to the first: "We should fear, love, and trust in God above all things." Luther simply echoes the Bible here. David confesses to the Lord, "Against You, You only, have I sinned" (Psalm 51:4), and Paul calls covetousness—a sin we don't worry much about, being last in the list—idolatry (Colossians 3:5). Straight from a minor number 10 to a major number 1. We all have some self-examination to do, considering our stations in life according to the Ten Commandments (Small Catechism, Confession)!

To "fear, love, and trust in God above all things" includes trusting His righteousness instead of our own. We do not point to the Law to justify ourselves as being better than the rest. Well, sometimes we do. Christians are accused of this all the time—and often we deserve it. But we must not use the Law to justify ourselves. That is most unlawful! We ought rather to point only to Jesus, who justifies us! Christ says, "I came not to call the righteous, but sinners" (Matthew 9:13), and He is the God "who justifies the ungodly" (Romans 4:5). We are yet totally sinners (according to our own selves) until we put off this body of flesh. But "if the Son sets you free, you will be free indeed" (John 8:36), so we are also totally saints, by His blood and say-so. This is what it means to be justified by faith.

This also means the life of a Christian is a life of continual repentance. Now, that life doesn't have to be dour and sad, but it finds new joy always in Jesus. That looks odd to the world. After all, who looks forward to repenting? But it's quite freeing! The fact that repentance goes hand-in-hand with faith and that our boast is not in being holier-than-thou but in Christ, who forgives us, may be a crucial surprise to our unbelieving neighbors, who try to scrape by, struggling to justify themselves. That's what life outside of Christ is, isn't it? And it's exhausting. There's a great opportunity for witness!

When we go to the "sinners and tax collectors" to tell them about Jesus, we should not "lord it over them" (Mark 10:42) as the righteous trying to train the unrighteous to be better (that is, more like us). That may be what they expect, but let it not be what they get! We should warn them of the sentence of God's righteous wrath, under which we also would be but for Christ (Luke 23:40). Then, when the Law has struck home, we should comfort them with the same comfort by which Christ has comforted us poor sinners (2 Corinthians 1:3–7; 5:16–21). For we are the ungodly just as they are, according to our natures, but we believe—as we invite them to—that we all are justified in Jesus' blood, by the God "who justifies the ungodly" (Romans 4:5).

When we are less than clear about the Law, when we act as if it condemns only some people and not us, we give an inaccurate witness about who Jesus is. We come off as holier-than-thou, boasting in ourselves and our good way of living, when our boast should be in Christ and His righteousness alone. Witnessing to our own sinfulness and need is the accurate witness to the Law of God. Witnessing aright to the Law, we do not stand aloof above the mess but follow the example of Jesus to be "numbered with the transgressors" (Isaiah 53:12; Mark 15:28) so as to present the Gospel clearly to them, that they might be, by faith in Christ, also numbered with us saints.

The Gospel: The Apostles' Creed

Just as the catechism helps us be accurate about the Law, so it does with the Gospel, following the Apostles' Creed. The Apostles' Creed is so named because it faithfully outlines the apostolic witness in phrases drawn practically verbatim from God's Word.

Luther divides the Creed into three articles, reflecting the Trinity: Father, Son, and Holy Spirit. Remember, this is the one and only and true God, as taught throughout the Bible from the beginning, though much more clearly drawn in the New Testament. Nor is this one and true God knowable in other forms, as, for example, the "Jehovah only" of the Jehovah's Witnesses; the god of modern-day Jews, which excludes Jesus; Allah, the god of Islam; the various gods of the East; or the "God for this world" of Mormonism, of whom they speak as Father, Son, Jesus, Spirit, and so on, but meaning something entirely different than what the Creed and Bible say. All who believe in such gods need our witness of the one true

God. Their gods force them to deal with their own sin and to work out their own salvation. The one true God made Himself man to save, and He gives us forgiveness, life, and salvation as a gracious gift. He is "the Lamb slain from before the foundation of the world" (Revelation 13:8, author's translation).

I had a seminary professor who shouted at his classes, "There is no god!" And no, he's not an atheist but a Lutheran! Maybe I should explain: What he meant was that there is no generic category of god containing "Holy Trinity" or "Allah" or whatever other gods, like chocolate could be Hershey or Nestle or Dove. There is one God, and He is Father, Son, and Holy Spirit, from and to all eternity, and revealed once and for all in the flesh in the person of Jesus Christ. Know Him, and you know God. Don't know Him, and you have no idea what "God" is—except, perhaps, that you should be afraid of Him. That is not faith (Large Catechism II 65–66).

Yet we're inundated by generic God talk. It's popular, because people disagree on who God is or don't really care about specifics. But it is also misleading because, apart from the Holy Trinity, "there is no 'god.' " If all we talk about is "God," it's likely to be heard generically. That will not lead people to know God as He is or to believe in Him. It might even

For a further investigation of the differences between Christianity and these and other religions, check out Adam Francisco's *One God, many gods* (available from CPH). This book identifies the central teachings of each and provides tools for Christians who encounter people of other faiths in their daily lives.

confirm a false faith in a generic god, who doesn't exist! Only Jesus opens the way of faith to the Father (John 14:6–7), and only the Spirit gives that faith (1 Corinthians 12:3).

The Creed presents this true God—Father, Son, and Holy Spirit—so that we may believe in Him, so that faith can "fear, love, and trust in God above all things" (Small Catechism, First Commandment). The Creed is not an eleventh commandment about what you have to believe, on top of all you have to do according to the other ten. Outsiders often think that way, that doctrine is yet another burden on top of good works. Rather, doctrine is the substance of the faith, and faith saves us. Doctrine shows us God as He is, inviting us to trust in Him. We can learn and speak it, not grudgingly, as some annoying or embarrassing burden, but with confidence and joy as a privilege, as the saving gift it is.

The Father and Creation

The Creed leads Luther to associate the Father with the work of creation (though the Son and the Spirit also certainly participate). He is "the Father Almighty, maker of heaven and earth." Going beyond the original creation, which sets God apart from all created things and establishes humankind's special relationship to God (Genesis 1–2), Luther speaks of God's continued providence for His creation, His sustaining of the world and you and everything. "All this," he says, "He does only out of fatherly, divine goodness and mercy, without any merit or worthiness in me" (Small Catechism, First

Article). "All this" includes body and soul, food and drink, house and home, and so much more. Everything!

As Christians, we know we receive our daily bread—everything we need—as a gift from a loving heavenly Father, for Christ has opened His Father's ear and heart to us. We therefore know, with Paul, the secret of contentment: to trust that everything God sends is for our good and that "I can do all things through Him who strengthens me" (Philippians 4:13; see also vv. 10–20; Hebrews 13:1–6; James 1:16–18). This remarkable hope frees us to live (as we'll discuss more in Chapter 4) for others and not for ourselves. Such living, in the midst of an otherwise pretty hopeless world, cannot help but be noticed and, God willing, questioned by our neighbors, to give us a chance to explain the "reason for the hope that is in you." (This isn't the first time you've seen that phrase from 1 Peter 3:15, and it won't be the last! It's a refrain in this book because it grasps so well our Christian witness.)

The Son and Redemption

The Creed's Second Article focuses on God's Son, Jesus Christ, and His work of redemption. The basic kernel of Luther's explanation, "Jesus is Lord," is the first Christian creed (Romans 10:9; 1 Corinthians 12:3).

When someone says, "Jesus is my Lord," *Lord* is often taken as "boss." "He tells me what to do, and I do it." You can imagine that unbelievers would think that's what it means. They don't know what it is to have a Savior, but they know what it is to have a boss. However, this is not what the Creed really means. To say "Jesus is Lord" is to confess that this man Jesus, born of the virgin Mary, crucified and buried, raised and ascended, is at the same time, in the same person, *the Lord*, the Son of God, one with the Father and Spirit in the one true and eternal God. More pointedly, to say "Jesus is Lord" is to say that He is the one true God, whom we are to "fear, love, and trust in . . . above all things"—even as sinners!

To this early creed, Luther adds the word *my*. He is my Lord. Jesus is who He is and does what He does—the devil himself knows that—but the "I believe" of faith also includes that "He is for me." My trust is in Him. He saves me. The heart of the Second Article is what Christ has done for me and for all: He "suffered under Pontius Pilate, was crucified, died and was buried. He descended into hell. The third day He rose again from the dead." Luther describes this heart of the Gospel in terms of a buying back, a redemption, of us as of empty pop cans, paid "not with gold or silver, but with His holy, precious blood and with His innocent suffering and death" (Small Catechism, Second Article). This is fact. This is finished. The debt is paid "for our sins, and not for ours only but also for the sins of the whole world" (1 John 2:2). Here the reason for the Father's pure grace is shown, despite our gravest and most staining sins: His only Son has died for us, in our place, and the debt is paid.

Thus I translate John 3:16—a good and memorable witness passage—as "for God loved the world in this way: that

He gave His only Son . . . " The giving of the Son into death is not the measure of how much, "so (much)," God loved the world. It is the means of God loving the world. The death and resurrection of Jesus is how He does it. The Creed is the unfolding not only of God's identity but also of His love.

The importance of this point cannot be overstated. Who has not wondered, "How can a loving God . . . ?" How many people said that after 9/11, or after hurricanes, floods, tornadoes, fires, droughts, accidents, crimes, or other tragedies? But here is a chance to witness where and how God loves the world, no matter what else befalls: He gives His Son into death for sin, and His Son rises victorious over death, bearing the victory for us. That is not an idea or philosophy, but fact. It is not complicated. You can explain that and speak the profound truth of God's love to the hurting!

Doing so, you would be bearing witness not to opinion or feeling, but to saving fact. The ground of faith—that we are redeemed, that God forgives our sins and loves us, that He extends to us His grace and works all things for good—is the resurrection of Jesus from the death that atoned for all sin. It is given to us, as Luther says, "just as He is risen from the dead, lives and reigns to all eternity" (Small Catechism, Second Article). The Christian faith rests on this fact to which you, by way of the apostolic record, bear witness. If He is not raised, we are still in our sins (1 Corinthians 15:14–17). But since He is, "this is most certainly true" (Small Catechism, Second Article).

The Spirit and Sanctification

The Third Article of the Creed reads most like a laundry list: Spirit, Church, saints, forgiveness, resurrection, life everlasting. Luther connects these beautifully to describe the work of the Third Person of the Trinity, the Holy Spirit. Luther describes His work as sanctification, in a broad sense, "making holy." Not "making more holy," as in making us better people (there is no "more holy," as we've said), though He does lead us to good works too. But He is primarily "making holy" as in "making completely holy," for Jesus' sake, by the forgiveness of sins, through faith.

Luther's explanation begins with a conundrum: "I believe that I cannot by my own reason or strength believe in Jesus Christ, my Lord, or come to Him; but the Holy Spirit has . . ." That Jesus has redeemed us is fact for faith to cling to. But where does this faith come from? That's a problem for fallen people, who'd rather run away from God than listen and repent and believe!

When Jesus Himself preached, He encountered opposition, not acceptance. After one sermon, practically everyone but the Twelve took off, angry, and Jesus asked the disciples if they would leave too (John 6:67). When He was on His way to the cross to work that great redemption, "they all left Him and fled" (Mark 14:50). They could not bear it, let alone believe it. The message that we cannot by ourselves overcome our sinfulness raises the ire of our fallen nature. We protest, "We have not been slaves!" even though our sins prove differently (John 8:31–36). We find forgiveness unfair, especially when it is extended equally to those who have sinned against us. That's what we are bound to do. Scripture does not teach free will in these matters. We are captives of the devil until Jesus sets us free (Epitome of the Formula of Concord II and Solid Declaration II).

Thus, faith does not originate in our decision for Jesus, which we cannot make of ourselves, but in the Holy Spirit. As Paul says, "No one can say 'Jesus is Lord' except in the Holy Spirit" (1 Corinthians 12:3). That is good, for what we do is never reliable, but what God does through His definite means always is. Luther's explanation of the Third Article unfolds this, and we'll speak more of these means—all focusing on the forgiveness of sins—in the next chapter.

What this means for witness is that we are not out to get someone to decide for Jesus or get someone to accept Jesus. We are proclaiming the powerful Word of God, through which the Holy Spirit promises to work, and then waiting for Him, where and when it pleases Him, through that Word, to create faith in Christ (Augsburg Confession V). That God Himself does creates faith for us, too, is purest and most certain Gospel.

Key Points

- Our witness, guided by the Small Catechism, must accurately reflect God's true Law and true Gospel.

- The Ten Commandments correct and complete the Law written in our hearts as a matter not only of hand and mouth but also of eye and heart.

- The Creed presents the one true God, is a memorable outline of the Gospel, and keeps us from speaking generically of God.

Discussion Questions

1. The Gospels present the saving facts about Jesus. How does this chapter's example from Mark help us to understand what to look for on every page of every Gospel? In terms of what critical event should we understand everything Jesus does and says?

2. How does Jesus speak of *all* the Scriptures (Luke 24:25–27, 44–47; John 5:39–40)? How does this insight help us witness to the true content of the Scriptures when we find people confused about them or taking them out of context (Acts 8:26–39)?

3. The Ten Commandments are fairly well-known but widely misunderstood. What does God intend them to do? Are they functioning properly in our minds if we can tick off the commandments we have kept and focus only on those we haven't?

4. Review the Ten Commandments and their explanations in the Small Catechism, and discuss for a few of them

how you might explain that God means us good—not to "step on our rights"—through these commandments, both in terms of the Law and in terms of Christ and faith.

5. With the Apostles' Creed and its catechism explanation before you, discuss how it would help you answer the simple, searching question, "Who is God?" (If it helps, imagine different people asking.)

6. Think of some examples of generic God talk you have seen or heard recently—or maybe even spoken or written yourself! Often, when a person is sick or has suffered a loss, we say, "God bless you" or "I'll pray for you." How might you speak less generically and provide a clearer witness? Where might you find the words? How might you practice?

Action Items

1. **Become a sermon connoisseur:** "Rightly handling the word of truth" (2 Timothy 2:15) to discern Law and Gospel is fundamental to the training of every Lutheran preacher and ought to be reflected in every sermon. The Law is to point out our sins, to bring us to repentance. The Gospel, which must win the day, is to point us to Christ's righteousness for us. Knowing to look for those two things, Law and Gospel, listen actively for how your pastor applies each. So that neither goes in

one ear and out the other, see if you can remember, or perhaps even discuss with your family, both the Law and the Gospel of the sermon on Sunday afternoon! Not only will it help your memory, but it will also add the ammunition of the Sunday sermon to your witnessing magazine!

2. **Become a Bible connoisseur:** The same Law/Gospel understanding can be applied to make your time in the Scriptures more rewarding. As you read your devotions, think, "Law: What is God telling me here I ought to be doing (or not doing), of what should I repent, and what must I change?" At the same time, think, "Gospel: What are God's promises to me here in Christ Jesus? How is He assuring me of forgiveness and drawing me to life made new by Him?" Keep in mind that if you're looking to the Law to save you or to the Gospel to whip you into shape, you're getting things confused! When you've read a passage, see if you can summarize what it means in terms of Law and Gospel.

3. **Keep Christ in Christmas:** Get a head start on your Christmas letter! Research Christmas, studying the Scriptures (Matthew 1–2; Luke 1–2; John 1) and good, sturdy hymns that get to the heart of what Christmas is about. Then write an introductory paragraph for your family and friends confessing why Christmas matters and how it is intended for them.

4. **Build an "old standby" file:** In a notebook or computer file, list the reasons you have to write cards, call friends, or send an e-mail. "Death in the family. Graduation. New Job. Baby," and so on. Organize it however works for you. When you run across a Bible passage, bit of a sermon, hymn stanza, or prayer or psalm that you think would be perfect for one of those occasions, file it! That way, when those times come where "you have to say something," you have some great and substantive material handy! The exercise may even train your brain to look for opportunities to speak a helpful and fitting word of truth.

So Jesus said to the Jews who had believed Him, "If you abide in My word, you are truly My disciples, and you will know the truth, and the truth will set you free." They answered Him, "We are offspring of Abraham and have never been enslaved to anyone. How is it that You say, 'You will become free'?" (John 8:31–33)

This chapter explores in more depth topics we might call "Lutheran distinctives"—topics Lutherans see differently from others who also may be (or may call themselves) Christians. When the Book of Concord, the collection of the Lutheran Confessions, was assembled in 1580, the Lutherans wrote in the preface, "we have not at all wished to create something new or to depart from the truth of the heavenly doctrine, which our ancestors . . . as well as we ourselves, have acknowledged and professed. We mean the doctrine that, having been taken from the prophetic and apostolic Scriptures, is contained (a) in the three ancient Creeds; (b) in the Augsburg Confession," and so on (Preface 23).

The same is our intent today, to bear witness before kings and emperors and the guy across the fence to the true doctrine of Christ and His apostles, as it is helpfully explained in our creeds and Confessions. When we do that, the world may call us worse than Lutherans, but let them call us what they will! "The Word they still shall let remain" (*LSB* 656:4).

There are many Christians who aren't Lutherans, but to be Lutheran is simply to be Christian, as best the Scriptures tell us how. So we will not shy away from these "Lutheran distinctives" in our witness.

The Lutheran Difference
Goes below the Surface, to the Very Core

We've already talked about things that make our witness as Lutherans distinctive. The last chapter was about two fundamental words of faith, Law and Gospel, organized around the Ten Commandments and the Apostles' Creed. We touched on the Law of God, God Himself, and how He redeemed us. You can't get more basic! Nevertheless, I don't think you'd have to go far to find people who consider themselves Christians but nonetheless disagree fundamentally with the little bit I've already said.

Mormons, for example, call themselves Christians but don't believe in the triune God. As we've seen, the Holy Trinity—Father, Son, and Holy Spirit—like the Bible and Creeds say, is the only true God, and that's the only way to know and worship Him. Everything else is idolatry. The simple truth is that not everything that calls itself Christian truth actually is. The devil is a liar, and where God builds a church, Satan puts up a chapel. Get used to it! This calls for discernment and the Word of God. Our witness, as our faith, must be accurate and precise. We have to be prepared to give a defense for our hope when it is challenged.

Even many who confess the Trinity would dispute salvation being by grace through faith in Jesus alone, apart from works. At the least they might say that folks can get to heaven by being good—in which case, they are not only adding works to faith but even throwing faith out altogether. But "by works of the law no human being will be justified" (Romans 3:20).

Some Christians feel that Christians would fall into debauchery if told justification is simply by faith, so they teach works are necessary too. They think perhaps Jesus gets us in by forgiveness but we stay in the kingdom by keeping the rules, more or less. This denies what Paul says (Romans 1:16–17), that the power of God is in the Gospel (not the Law) for full salvation. This is also less than truthful about God Himself, "who justifies the ungodly" (Romans 4:5).

Others think one can keep on indulging in, promoting, and boasting of what the Bible calls grave and deadly sins and still be a Christian. They ignore the fact that Christ came not to justify sins but to justify sinners and "to destroy the works of the devil" (1 John 3:8). Paul says, "Those who do such things will not inherit the kingdom of God" (Galatians 5:21), and Christ Himself says, "Go, and from now on sin no more" (John 8:11).

None of these adjustments to the simple truth of justification by faith alone are right, because Christ and the Bible teach otherwise. We cannot paper over such differences in our witness or act as if they don't matter. On this topic of justification by faith, identified by the Lutheran reformers as "the article on which the Church stands or falls," we have not an inch of flexibility. But that's good!

We know the truth. It is sweetest Gospel for those terrified by their sins and fleeing to a Savior in Christ Jesus: "Our churches teach that people cannot be justified before God by their own strength, merits, or works. People are freely justified for Christ's sake, through faith, when they believe that they are received into favor and that their sins are forgiven for Christ's sake. By His death, Christ made satisfaction for our sins. God counts this faith for righteousness in His sight (Romans 3 and 4)" (Augsburg Confession IV). That is good news, the greatest news!

The Augsburg Confession then moves on, as does the Creed, to outline how this faith comes about and is sustained by the definite working of God the Holy Spirit through definite means: "So that we may obtain this faith, the ministry of

We are in good company—when presenting the truth of justification by faith alone to the Christians in Galatia, Paul neither flexed nor gave an inch. For more on this, see Paul's Letter to the Galatians.

teaching the Gospel and administering the Sacraments was instituted. Through the Word and Sacraments, as through instruments, the Holy Spirit is given. He works faith, when and where it pleases God, in those who hear the good news" (Augsburg Confession V 1–2).

Points of doctrine such as justification by faith are often called Lutheran distinctives, and so they are, because many Christians do not believe them or at least don't talk about them. That doesn't mean our witness needs to be shy about them—in fact, they are essential to keeping our witness true. Remember my professor who shouted, "There is no god," meaning that there was no generic idea of God? We might as well shout, "There is no generic Christianity!" Everyone has to take some position on what the Bible says on the many issues that divide the various denominations, sects, and cults that still call themselves Christian. Even to decide to have no opinion is to have an opinion—that it couldn't matter less. And neither "yes" nor "no" sides, nor the Lord, would agree with that. Either "thus says the Lord," or He doesn't.

Our pastors swear to teach in accord with the Book of Concord because these things teach what the Lord has said. Once you have a solid understanding of the catechism, you might grow even more in Christian doctrine, for faith and witness, by plumbing the precise and practical theology of our written Confessions, which your pastor can help you find. In a confusing time, with many denominations, sects, and cults going by the name *Christian*, our Lutheran Confessions point out that many who consider themselves Christian aren't. There are many more who are, at best, at grave risk of fumbling what God means to give by His definite promises, because they have much of the message wrong. There's an opportunity for truthful and patient and loving witness, if ever there was one! But to give it, we must know accurately the way of God (Acts 18:26; Ephesians 4:11–16).

Is It God's Work or Ours?

Often, we think the Christian witness is to try to get someone to make a decision for Jesus or to accept Jesus. Evangelism tracts and hotel Bibles often have a decision page that encourages a sinner to pray a prayer and sign on the dotted line. Americans, I suppose, like this sort of thing, with our emphasis on freedom and voting and choice, but it flies in the face of what we confessed of the Third Article of the Creed: "I cannot by my own reason or strength believe."

No one, of his or her own free will, chooses Jesus. Rather, the Holy Spirit overcomes a will that was captive to the devil and bestows faith instead, as a gift from God. Focusing on a human decision obscures this crucial fact of salvation. What we have done is always suspect. Did you really decide for Jesus this time? How do you know? The flesh is weak. What God has done by Word and Sacrament is sure. This might be called a Lutheran distinctive, because many Christians would rather focus on the decision. But for us, it is simply what Christ and His apostles teach—and we ought not forget it or act as if it weren't important!

The last three chief parts of the catechism speak of the Sacraments, in which God acts on us to create and sustain faith and to forgive sins. Here you might say, "Whoa! What do Sacraments have to do with witnessing? Not all Christians agree on this stuff, so what's the point of getting into it?" But there is a point, or two!

First, so what if not all Christians agree? We have the truth, from Scripture, about how God works through Sacraments to save us. Our faith is meant to cling firmly to them, even if other Christians try to limp along without them, or at least without their fullness. Second, they are not done in secret. Outsiders see or at least know of them. Rather than treat the Sacraments like embarrassing things we'd rather not discuss, we ought to be prepared to explain them. They offer hidden opportunities to get to the heart of the matter, the fact that salvation is God's work, not ours, by grace received through faith that He Himself gives us, so that "the promise may rest on grace and be guaranteed" (Romans 4:16).

Holy Baptism

The world understands the desire for a new start and the commitment to a new and better approach. We expect tearful apologies from our stumbling stars of sports, stage, and state. We venture annual New Year's resolutions with great gusto, and sometimes they last a week or two. It's largely a show. It's quite natural to explain to someone the ritual of Baptism as many do: as an outward sign of an inward change of will, a new commitment to follow the covenant or Law, to choose Jesus as your Lord. The world might understand that and take it as another pious show—and they'd be right. Such a baptism is robbed of its promise and power, which is "to all who believe this, as the words and promises of God declare," that "it works forgiveness of sins, rescues from death and the devil, and gives eternal salvation" (Small Catechism, Baptism, Second Part).

In real Baptism, God is working, washing, renewing, and regenerating (Titus 3:5–8). The starkest demonstration of that fact is that we baptize infants, who don't ask for it or make any promises (except through sponsors). We simply trust the Word of God that Baptism is for all nations, including their infants (Matthew 28:19) and that "the promise [of Baptism] is for you and for your children" (Acts 2:39). That means most of us Lutherans don't have a gripping testimonial or conversion story as many others have. Such stories usually focus on a person's decision for Jesus because they're trying to get someone else to decide for Jesus. But our conversion, our salvation, doesn't rest on a decision of ours but on the work of the Holy Spirit, who gave us faith—for most of us, before we could even tell anyone what faith was. How do we know? Because the Word of God says so.

The fact is that Baptism is not a sign of your decision or commitment; rather, it is God's own working and claim on you. This is important not just for babies or on the day you were baptized, for the promise of Baptism always, always remains for you to return to it in repentance and faith and be restored as God's own. "The Old Adam in us," the Small Catechism says, "should by daily contrition and repentance be drowned and die with all sins and evil desires, and . . . a new man should daily emerge and arise to live before God in righteousness and purity forever" (Small

Explore what God says about the power of Holy Baptism to create saving faith in Matthew 28:19; Mark 16:16; Titus 3:5–8; Romans 6:4. Also, see the Small Catechism on Baptism.

Catechism, Baptism, Fourth Part). Since God does it, it is sure. As Luther says elsewhere, "Our Baptism abides forever" (Large Catechism IV 77).

Our culture talks a lot about self-esteem, and people try all sorts of ways to defend their self-image against damage from without and within. We should be careful about that. We are made in the image of God, yes (Genesis 1:26). But "let anyone who thinks that he stands take heed lest he fall" (1 Corinthians 10:12), and "if anyone thinks he is something, when he is nothing, he deceives himself" (Galatians 6:3). The Christian has a different identity, in something more sure than the façades we build around our own fragile self-esteem. Our identity is established by God, in God, in God's own name in Baptism. This identity abides forever and stands against human enemies and devils. Luther said that in his deepest despairs and temptations, he relied on the words "I am baptized!" And so may we!

We have been buried by Baptism with Christ into death that we may also walk with Him in newness of life (Romans 6:1–4). Baptism calls us always to repentance—it is, after all, "for the remission of sins." But when so called to repentance (and the catechism says daily, at least!), we are reminded that here a new person comes forth by God's working, to live before Him in righteousness and purity forever. That identity the world cannot take away is a strange hope the world may find worth asking about—and one you can now explain from God's Word!

Confession (and Let's Not Forget Absolution)

Someone remarked to me years ago that the Divine Service would be much more comfortable for newcomers if we did away with "I, a poor, miserable sinner . . ." at the outset (*LSB*, p. 184). I suppose it might be. A trip to the dentist would also be more comfortable without the tooth scraping, but then, why go?

Asking for total forgiveness implies that one is a total sinner, and unless faith in Christ is ready to catch us, that's a leap no one's itching to take. Yet, for us who believe in Christ and His forgiveness of sins, we find here a great comfort and treasure: "Absolution, that is, forgiveness, from the pastor as from God Himself, not doubting, but firmly believing that by it our sins are forgiven before God in heaven" (Small Catechism, Confession).

The place of the general Confession and Absolution at the beginning of the Divine Service reminds us that "everything . . . in the Christian Church is ordered toward this goal: we shall daily receive in the Church nothing but the forgiveness of sin through the Word and signs [Sacraments], to comfort and encourage our consciences as long as we live here" (Large Catechism II 55).

Visitors to the Divine Service sometimes find it shocking that a pastor forgives sins. They might be even more shocked to hear that the catechism and Lutheran Church also speak of individual or private Confession and Absolution, in which troubled sinners confess to their pastors particular sins and hear forgiveness specifically their own, so that they may have every confidence that the sins that most trouble them are indeed forgiven and put away. They may be shocked at a man speaking forgiveness—"Who is he to forgive sins?" Or they may be shocked at the idea of free forgiveness altogether—"Why should those sins just be forgiven?"

The answer in both cases is Jesus, who died for the sins of the entire world (1 John 2:2), who commanded "that repentance and forgiveness of sins should be proclaimed in His name to all nations" (Luke 24:47), and who established the Office of the Keys so that His people could hear and believe the precious word of freedom from their sins in His blood (John 20:21–23). If, from our own study of the Scriptures and the Confessions, we are prepared to explain, their surprise or consternation might be turned to a scriptural witness of who Jesus is, and who He is for us, and what is the purpose of the Church.

The Sacrament of the Altar

Likewise, the Sacrament of the Altar is often thought of as posing problems for our witness to visitors in the Divine Service. Here, also, a little preparation on your part goes a long way. Luther's presentation of the Lord's Supper is not complicated. All he does is stick with the words of Jesus: that it is His body and blood because He says so, and He is Lord; that it is for the forgiveness of sins; and that it requires faith, "for the words 'for you' require all hearts to believe" (Small Catechism, Sacrament of the Altar). Lutherans didn't invent some strange "Lutheran doctrine of the Lord's Supper." We simply listen to Jesus and to Paul.

Because the true body and true blood of God's Son in the Lord's Supper are the most precious and powerful substances on earth, Paul warns us that we should be united in doctrine and life before the altar. Those who do not discern the body, those who bring division (in doctrine or life), or those who are not there for the forgiveness of sins are in danger of sinning against or of being "guilty concerning the body and blood of the Lord" (1 Corinthians 11:27; see also vv. 17–34), and they should not receive. This practice of closed Communion is often perceived as off-putting to visitors, but it is what our Lord has given us, and it can be turned to an opportunity for witness. It testifies that what is going on here is no human show or empty symbol but a divine Means of Grace, the real presence of Christ's true body and blood, which must be regarded with all seriousness. God Himself is working here, in life-and-death matters—for life, we pray, for repentant sinners, who come not on their merit or terms, but on our Lord's!

Access to the Sacrament needs to be addressed with respect and gentleness, moving from shock, disappointment, or griping about closed Communion to a meaningful witness about the Lord's Supper, the Lord behind it, and the reality of His Church, which He desires to be one in doctrine (Ephesians 4:1–16). This is by no means beyond the capability of any Christian armed with the Small Catechism and 1 Corinthians 11. A great goal to work toward is getting your friend who has questions to seek instruction from the pastor, which, we pray, will lead him or her to confess our faith, the faith, and receiving with us all our Lord's precious gifts.

Key Points

- To be Lutheran is simply to be Christian. The Lutheran distinctives are not to be avoided in our witness to outsiders but used to give it clarity and the power of God's Word.

- The catechism prepares us to explain from God's Word the means by which God forgives sins and creates and strengthens faith.

- Holy Baptism is the foundational identity of the Christian and the base of our worth before God and one another: we are baptized into Christ Jesus.

- Confession and Absolution witness to the heart of the faith and purpose of the Church: the forgiveness of sins.

- The Lord's Supper and our practice of closed Communion is an accurate presentation of the doctrine of the Lord's Supper and the Gospel.

Discussion Questions

1. Sometimes we think justification is a topic for intellectuals. But it's not! How do we use the words *justify* or *justification*, *right* or *righteous*, or *make right* in common

speech? Where do these concepts come into play in daily life? How can these be opportunities to think or speak about what Jesus does for us?

2. What's the harm in teaching a person to make a decision for Jesus or to accept Jesus into his or her heart, or saying that a person has to be really sure he or she is not going to do it again before believing that he or she has forgiveness? People relate to this sort of language, but how does the catechism (reflecting the Bible) speak about our coming to faith and the forgiveness of our sins? [Hint: This question looks back to the Third Article of the Creed.]

3. How might our study of justification and the Sacraments help you address the following made-up characters? Brainstorm what you might say or, if you like, role-play some situations:

    a. You see Bob again at the diner. You know he's got a cross tattooed on his arm and a girlfriend at home and that he doesn't go to church. When you've asked, he says he prefers to keep his faith in Jesus "childlike."

    b. Jessica, whom you last saw when she was confirmed, comes back from college pregnant and without a boyfriend. Her mom wants her to get back to church but says Jessica's worried what everyone will think, and she doesn't know what to say.

c. Betty says, "You Lutherans! If you tell them Baptism and faith save them, you'll never see them again."

d. Zachary came to church with your kids for the first time—probably anywhere. He watched everyone going so seriously to Communion, receiving a bit of bread and wine. You saw he was puzzled. What might you ask or explain as your family drives him home?

e. Okay, you get the hang of it! Have some fun and make up your own scenarios. Remember, this is a learning exercise!

4. What role do you find baptismal identity playing in your life of faith or your family members' lives of faith? How might you work on making it a more prominent part of your devotional life? What effects might your neighbors see and wonder about?

5. Read the Small Catechism on Baptism, Confession, and the Sacrament of the Altar. Think of some questions that might come up when those unfamiliar with your church observe these things, and practice giving good, understandable, biblical answers from the catechism.

Action Items

1. Martin Luther, as an aged pastor, professor, and reformer, said that he remained daily in the Small Catechism, always learning and being refreshed by

it in the truth. Make a plan to include a bit of the catechism in your daily devotions, perhaps taking as long as a month. You might, for example, follow Luther's "garland of four strands" to meditate and pray on (a) what it is teaching, (b) what to thank God for in what He is giving here, (c) what failings or laments to confess to God with regard to this point of teaching, and (d) what to pray for on the basis of what this teaching promises.

2. Go through the Small Catechism again, thinking not only of yourself and your situation but also of your Christian witness to others. Try to think of a conversation or situation where each chunk of the catechism might have helped you know what to say or do, or where it might prove useful in the future. This may help you to reflect on—in the light of God's Word and doctrine—and focus your witness to Jesus by word and deed.

3. Think of someone you know from your congregation— or even, especially, a family member—who hasn't been to church in a while. Call or write a note encouraging him or her to come back, witnessing to what you get out of the Divine Service, and hoping for him or her to receive with you. Or think about how you could gently and with respect work on him or her over time with what you've learned from this study. Stick to it! He or she is worth it!

4. Beg, borrow, or purchase a copy of Luther's Large Catechism (or if you're really blessed, a copy of *Concordia: The Lutheran Confessions*, which contains it and other great material). Read the Large Catechism, which is based on a collection of sermons organized around five of the Six Chief Parts of the Small Catechism (Confession is treated in passing as repentance in the Baptism part). These sermons on basic Christian doctrine are full of material for sharpening and focusing your witness. Make notes and discuss what you find with your family or a conversation partner.

You are the salt of the earth, but if salt has lost its taste, how shall its saltiness be restored? It is no longer good for anything except to be thrown out and trampled under people's feet. You are the light of the world. A city set on a hill cannot be hidden. Nor do people light a lamp and put it under a basket, but on a stand, and it gives light to all in the house. In the same way, let your light shine before others, so that they may see your good works and give glory to your Father who is in heaven. (Matthew 5:13–16)

We bear witness with more than words, in fact, with our very lives. This may sound like what's sometimes called lifestyle witnessing, presenting a picture before our neighbors of what saved people look like and hoping that they'll like it and want to be saved people too. In essence, the program is to try to look holy (whatever an attractive version of holy is) or even to try to look blessed. Dress for success!

Of course, our Lord says, "Beware of practicing your righteousness before other people in order to be seen by them" (Matthew 6:1). The "dress for success" evangelism program ("do what we do, and you can be successful like us!") was basically that of the Pharisees. This becomes mere show, and our neighbors can easily sniff out our hypocrisy (which means, literally, play-acting).

What does a genuinely Christian life look like, anyway? Isaiah says that our Lord Himself wasn't particularly attractive, humanly speaking (Isaiah 52:13–53:12), but bruised and bloodied. Yet, "with His wounds we are healed" (Isaiah 53:5). Likewise, in the Beatitudes, Jesus gives us some ideas of what Christian life looks like; it doesn't necessarily look like blessed living, but it is (Matthew 5:2–12). Blessedness is hidden under opposites, wrapped, humanly speaking, in a conundrum, a mystery.

That is how the kingdom of God works (1 Corinthians 1:18–31). Jesus' holiness and the righteousness of God are not put on display in a life merely of great works so that wise and upstanding people might want to be even more like Him. No! The righteousness of God is this: that He stoops to enter His own creation and live as one of us, is baptized and numbered with sinners, and bears our sins to the cross to die in our place so that sinners should flee to Him and be forgiven. In the ugliest event of human history, the crucifixion, the sinner's death of the one righteous man—such a great paradox—the forgiveness of sin and life everlasting was being wrought, once and for all, from on high.

What about our lives? Aren't we supposed to draw people to Jesus by our living? Yes. We are the salt of the earth, the city on a hill, the light on a stand. But this is not an artificial, distinct activity, a show we put on. It happens organically, without our even thinking about it, when we live by faith. It looks not attractive but goofy to the world—perhaps goofy enough that they will ask about the hope that drives such a life (1 Peter 3:15 yet again), and we can move in witness from puzzling, loving deeds to saving words.

Luther and the "Circuit Training" of the Christian Life

When Luther speaks of the Christian life, he speaks of three components. I'll share the Latin with you so you might remember the rhyme or at least impress your barber:

- *oratio*, prayer (in God's promises);

- *meditatio*, meditation (on God's Word);

- and *tentatio*, affliction or suffering (in godly living).

These three, he says, make a theologian—and by that he means a Christian, one who hears God's Word and speaks the truth to and about God. Not every Christian is a pastor, but for Luther, every Christian is a theologian!

These three form a cycle, almost like "circuit training." We pray for help on the basis of God's promises (*oratio*), for which we delve into His Word (*meditatio*). There we find promises but also how to live in love. Trying to live in love, we suffer (*tentatio*). Suffering, we despair of ourselves and are driven to repent and to pray for God's help, which sends us again to His Word to search out His promises in Christ, and so on, round and round. That is what it looks like to live as saint and sinner, constantly repenting of our sin but constantly justified by faith, and as such, expecting only good from God in heaven, even His Holy Spirit (Luke 11:11–13).

Perhaps this sounds uncomfortable—even dizzying—but that's where Christ has us for our good and our neighbors' good, going round and round in repentance and faith, putting off the old and putting on the new as long as we live, being conformed over and over to the image of the One who has redeemed us by His blood to "be His own and live under Him . . . in everlasting righteousness, innocence, and blessedness" (Small Catechism, Second Article; see also Colossians 3).

This looks funny to the world, and that's a good thing! Like the Pharisees, we do not do the things the heathen do, but neither do we boast of our ethical achievements or holy lives; rather, we boast in Christ. Others justify themselves, even when their works are evil. We flee to Christ for Him to justify us, even when, by the power of His Holy Spirit, our works turn out to be good. The world is willing to suffer nothing for anyone, having no one promising to bless. We suffer all for everyone, counting it a blessing to share in the sufferings of our Lord and having unfailing hope in the God who even raises the dead that He works all things for our good and gives us all we need purely by grace. Don't you think living like that might get you noticed?

So the Christian life ought to be! But it never quite is, is it? Paul says, not just to some Jewish-Christian bad eggs in Rome, but also to us, "The name of God is blasphemed among the Gentiles because of you" (Romans 2:24). For we have not lived this way, even toward one another. Likewise, our Lord says, "A new commandment I give to you, that you love one another: just as I have loved you, you also are to love one another. By this all people will know that you are My disciples, if you have love for one another" (John 13:34–35). I don't remember the last time someone took me aside and said, "I can see that you are different. You love like no one else in this world loves. You must be one of Jesus' disciples!" Maybe they just don't notice, or maybe my love is not so extraordinary as I thought. Maybe I'm not alone in that.

Repent. Part of the reason we don't have opportunities to speak the Gospel to the neighbors we love and want to hear the Gospel is that we haven't been very good at really loving them, and they have had no reason to ask about our hope. Repent, but don't despair. Remember the circuit training. Your love is for your neighbor's sake, not for your conscience's sake. Christ is for your conscience, and He loves you, and His work, unlike yours, is finished. You are forgiven, renewed by the One who makes all things new. Don't hang onto your guilt—let Him take it. Don't be afraid to try again, for He'll be there. Your neighbors need you.

So we live with Paul (Romans 7–8) in repentance and faith. Round and round we go, but faith clings to Christ, and He has won the victory. That's the hope on which the whole cycle turns, the fixed point that keeps us from getting dizzy and falling out of it. Faith clings to that hope in Christ, that in Him God fights for us and has won. What is there to do, then, but live for love by faith? Living in faith, by that hope, you will be noticed!

The Lord's Prayer
as the Cry of the Hope That Is in Us

Luther's approach to the Lord's Prayer in the catechism, the one chief part we haven't looked at yet, is to see it as the cry of that faith in the Christian life—a prayer offered in our hope. Christ gives it to us (Matthew 6:9–13) so we can have definite words to pray, knowing that His Father will answer us, even when we can hardly string our own two words together. Our Lord's Prayer runs contrary to every human idea of prayer, and unless our Lord had given it, we'd never dare to pray it. For how does He begin? "Our Father," He says. You can't go to a random guy on the street and say, "Hey, Dad! Give me lunch!" Indeed, the random guy on the street is by no means a god, let alone the one true God. Who would dare to approach God in heaven that way?

Well, we would. Don't lose sight of the surprise of that! We do so not because we are so bold, so worthy, or so darn lovable but because Jesus, God's Son, has redeemed us and by Baptism has made us children of the living God. We do not have to bargain or plead, cajole or compromise. We come on Jesus' merit and ask "as dear children ask their dear father" (Small Catechism, Lord's Prayer, Introduction). We ask all we need from our dear Father in heaven: for bread, that is, everything we need to support this body and life, for free by grace; for forgiveness, again, without proving we've earned it; for victory over temptation; and for deliverance from evil. We pray that His name be holy among us, that we might call upon it in every trouble, pray, praise and give thanks; and that His kingdom and will, both working for our good, might come among us also, "on earth as in heaven." It's a tall order to ask for everything by grace, free because Christ has paid for it! Then, to top it all, we say "amen," that is, "Yes, yes, it shall be so" (Small Catechism, the Lord's Prayer, Conclusion).

Why the amen? What makes us sure the prayer will be heard? Are we confident to add our amen because we have found just the right words to pray, have offered just the right bargain to God, or have cleaned ourselves to the point where He'd be willing to listen to us? No! We pray Jesus' words on Jesus' merit. In the same breath, we ask for blessings and to be forgiven. That is the prayer Jesus teaches, to call upon God, through Him, as those justified by faith alone. We are to expect, to trust without doubting, that for Christ's sake God will hear us and give all that is good. This is what it means to pray in Jesus' name (John 14:13–14), not that every prayer has to end with those words. To pray in Jesus' name is the prayer of those justified in Christ Jesus. To pray in Jesus' name is your prayer as God's forgiven child. Therefore, your hope is not just for forgiveness someday but for everything now. Not only our consciences, then, are freed by Christ, but also our hands and mouths and hearts, to love and serve our neighbor—because God Himself provides for us.

One final note on the Lord's Prayer and witness: prominent in the middle is the Fifth Petition, "Forgive us our trespasses as we forgive those who trespass against us." We said before that our forgiveness rests on the death and resurrection of Jesus, which atoned not only for our sins but also for the sins of the whole world. If that is true, then our witness to Him should call a thing what it is: namely, sins against us are called forgiven. Christ has paid for them—all of them. Christians ought not bear grudges. In fact, we pray against ourselves in the Lord's Prayer if we do, and we torture our own faith, which has a hard enough time believing that we are forgiven anyway, without our holding on to some sins. If we do not hold grudges in this world of grudge-bearers, our hope should especially be noticeable.

A Witness in Prayer

Prayer is not primarily given for witnessing, any more than the Divine Service is. Jesus gives prayer its own command and promise. It is not for show. If we pray simply for show, we are hypocrites, play-actors. We are so especially if we pray in a generic way, so as not to put off people around us who might believe in different gods.

But when we are asked to pray at a luncheon or with a friend in trouble or whenever, we can pray in a way that clearly reflects the theology and promise of prayer that Jesus gave. That's the way we should always pray. If we can't find our own words, His aren't bad; He said, "Pray then like this" (Matthew 6:9). Luther's Small Catechism also gives some worthy suggestions on prayer at morning, evening, and meals.

Praying confidently in both repentance and faith to a well-known Holy Trinity on the basis of Christ and His promises could lead someone to ask why you pray so differently from the "yearning masses," struggling to find a gracious god to get their petitions heard. That would give you a chance to explain—you know where I am going with this—the reason for the strange hope that is in you. Or perhaps, in conversation, you might be able to explain the familiar words of the Lord's Prayer, with some help from the catechism, to a friend in a way totally new to them and chock-full of the Good News of Jesus!

A Word about Vocation, Calling

I've said witnessing is not a separate "go and do it" activity. It is an organic part of your Christian life, in which God has called you to many vocations. *Vocation* is a Latin word for "calling." We tend to think of a calling as a profession or life's work. It is life's work, but I like to think of it as our faith hearing God's voice calling, through the neighbor, for us to love and serve. As Jesus says, "As you did it to one of the least of these My brothers, you did it to Me" (Matthew 25:40).

You likely have many of these vocation "hats," some more obvious and permanent than others. God gave you to parents; through them God said or says, "Honor your father and your mother" (Fourth Commandment). Perhaps you have siblings, a spouse, or children. You are a citizen of a country, a state, and a member of some community. You may have a job through which you serve your neighbor and are paid to serve your family, or you may volunteer to serve for those who can't pay or to do what no one will pay for. You have a family of faith in your congregation, mothers and sisters and brothers, now in this life, and you care for one another as members of the same body—at least you should (1 Corinthians 12:12–31; Galatians 6:10). You probably have a pastor, whom you are to hear and care for. That's a vocation too.

Luther's Table of Duties in the back of the catechism goes to the Bible to see what God says about how we are to live and love in our vocations. "Consider your place in life," he also says, "according to the Ten Commandments" (Small Catechism, Confession). The place where God has put you is important, and He doesn't mean for you to abandon caring for your children and teaching them the faith to go witness to some heathen somewhere. He's put you wherever you are for a reason. Your witness to Christ is largely living by faith where He has put you. At the same time, not all of these cries for help are permanent or obvious ones. When Jesus was asked, "Who is my neighbor?" (Luke 10:29), He turned it around: "Which of these . . . proved to be a neighbor to the man?" It was "the one who showed him mercy" (vv. 36–37). You can't do it all, but that's okay. In Christ, "it is finished" (John 19:30). You live by faith in Him, not by your crossed-off checklist.

Likewise, in our corporate life as congregations, where has God put you? Who are your neighbors? What are they suffering? How are we living before them (Colossians 4:5–6)? Do they know we care, or do we seem to be eyeing them scornfully from our own little lifeboat, waiting for the flood? These questions are important as we think about our witness. God may be calling to us through them to come and help.

Think about vocation as hearing the voice of God in the (maybe often silent) cries of your neighbors for help and then helping them—not just for a paycheck or because you want to keep busy, but because they need it.

That makes a difference in what we will do, for what compensation, and in how we will go about it. It may seem that you work for a paycheck to put food on your own table and to keep a roof over your head. Or if you do something that doesn't bring a paycheck, you must be working for some reward: to be praised as a doer of good, to earn stars in your crown in heaven, to be favored by a God who rewards good works, or to have that good feeling down inside at having done right, which is said to be its own reward.

It seems pretty obvious that we work in view of returns, pay, or rewards. None of that is living by faith. Faith sees and acts on another reality: that God, in fact, gives you all you need and enjoy for free, as a gift. That is not obvious to reason, but it is what faith believes and what we confess in the Creed's First Article, as Luther explains it in the Small Catechism: "He richly and daily provides me with all that I need to support this body and life. He defends me against all danger and guards and protects me from all evil. All this He does only out of fatherly, divine goodness and mercy, without any merit or worthiness in me."

To live by faith is to look first to God for all good and then to look to serving your neighbors. "Whatever your hand finds to do" (that is within your office, your station in life—don't go doing brain surgery or filling prescriptions if you're not qualified), "do it with your might" (Ecclesiastes 9:10), simply because your neighbors need it done, and God put you here to do it and would love them through you.

So living, you bear living witness to your Lord, who "came not to be served but to serve, and to give His life as a ransom for many" (Matthew 20:28). You are, like Paul's Corinthians, the apostles' living letter (2 Corinthians 3:1–2), a witness written by the apostolic doctrine to the world. You follow in the train of the martyrs, who not only spoke of Jesus but also took up His cross to follow Him. This martyrdom, witness by life as well as mouth, is not optional for the Christian but is an essential, organic part of the life that really is by faith (Romans 12; James 2:14–18; 1 John 3:16–18). By such a life, you bear Christ's witness before the world with more than words, so that, as the Holy Spirit provides opportunity, you may move with gentleness and respect (1 Peter 3:8–17) from deed to word, from love to hope, and explain how your love is not all there is. Rather, far better, God has loved the world by sending His only Son.

Key Points

- Lutherans' unique take on the Christian life flows from being justified by faith and receiving all things by grace, resting in Christ's promise, not in our progress.

- Our way of life and theology of prayer are part of our witness.

- God has put us in specific vocations or stations in life where He means us to stay and do our duty in service and witness to others.

Discussion Questions

1. When you flip through the channels and see the television preachers, what do you see in terms of the type of Christian life portrayed? If you listen, what kind of advice do they give? What do they promise? We might not watch this stuff—I rather hope we don't, except to know what's out there—but others might and be confused. What will our neighbors see in us that they won't be used to seeing there? What difference might that make?

2. Christians are often reluctant to admit or show their shortcomings to unbelieving friends, lest they be put off. Of course, just because they don't have the faith doesn't mean they don't have any sense. They probably notice anyway. How might we go about using those failings, flounderings, and frustrations and how we deal with them to show the essence of our faith?

3. Outside of the general Confession and Absolution in the service on Sunday, how does repentance and forgiveness (reconciliation) pop up in your life? How do you or how might you enact the vital reality of daily dying and rising in Christ which the catechism talks about?

4. What does this reconciliation and reconciling (2 Corinthians 1:3–7) have to do with your unbelieving neighbors, and what impact might it have on them? When they sin against you, are those sins to be forgiven—or are they forgiven already? How do they find out? How might this point to your strange hope?

5. Read the Small Catechism on the Lord's Prayer. The First, Second, and Third petitions, I think, have non-obvious explanations but very good ones. As we race through these "most sinned against words on earth" (as Luther called them because we race through them so), what are we praying for and against? We say, "On earth as it is in heaven." We ask for these things to be a reality among us now. What does this mean for our Christian lives? What does this have to do with our witness to who God is?

6. As a pastor, folks often ask me when I'm out and about to pray for them. If I have time, I question why they don't feel they can pray themselves—not that I don't want to pray for them, but I want to get to the point that God means us to pray in faith, on Christ's merits, not on the basis of our own personal worthiness. Think of an opportunity you've had recently to pray with someone in trouble or when you heard someone else pray for a group. Discuss how you might pray in some of these situations, (1) specifically to the God we know and trust (none of that generic God-talk!), (2) on the basis

of God's definite promises, and (3) in both repentance and faith that Christ has opened to you the Father's ear. Discuss how you might explain to someone who heard you why you prayed as you did.

Action Items

1. An earlier chapter mentioned setting aside time for daily devotions in the catechism. I hope you've chosen to do that, both for your own faith and for the sake of your witness. Now that you know about *oratio, meditatio,* and *tentatio,* perhaps that devotional time is a good time to think on that explicitly each day, to keep yourself refreshed in Christ in the cycle of the Christian life. You, your neighbors, and your witness might benefit.

2. With your family or close friends, talk about this cycle of the Christian life. When sin stirs the pot, how is it resolved among you? Are you explicit about repentance and forgiveness? Do you remind one another that sin is already forgiven in Christ Jesus and that you consider your own grudges to be wrong and want to be rid of them? It may be a little silly, but my wife and I have the habit of asking each other for a "new moment" when one realizes the other's been wronged. That's our shorthand for "Christ covers it, and this is, right now, the new day the Lord has made." What's your family's shorthand? If you don't have one, may I recommend you figure one out? As we are reconciled to God, so we are to be reconciled with one another and to learn to

be reconciling people. This absolutely critical witness starts best at home!

3. Take stock of the Table of Duties in the back of the Small Catechism and other passages of the catechism or Bible that have to do with vocations to which God has called you. Set aside some time to "consider your place in life according to the Ten Commandments." Who have been your neighbors; that is, to whom have you shown mercy? Which neighbors might be calling for your attention? Where have you withheld mercy or love or service because you were waiting for personal advantage? What impact has this had on your witness to Christ in how you live? Repent and believe the Gospel! If this kind of self-evaluation troubles you or this kind of giving life exhausts you, go and let your pastor serve you, refreshing you in the forgiveness of sins and promises of Christ—that is his vocation, after all!

4. Help your congregation take stock of community needs around you. Where are people suffering or in need? Locked up? Hungry? Lonely? What challenges face your community? Are parents looking for help teaching their small children, or are there young mothers who need a helping hand? How can you reach out to your neighbors with the love of Christ—not as an advertising campaign or fund-raising or membership drive—but simply because they need mercy? Then, how in that service could you make that crucial step from deed to Word?

Now who is there to harm you if you are zealous for what is good? But even if you should suffer for righteousness' sake, you will be blessed. Have no fear of them, nor be troubled, but in your hearts honor Christ the Lord as holy, always being prepared to make a defense to anyone who asks you for a reason for the hope that is in you; yet do it with gentleness and respect. (1 Peter 3:13–15)

In every age the Church has her challenges,

and I suppose every age wonders, "How long, O LORD?" (Psalm 13:1). She always lives in the last days. Christ has come, died, is risen, and the world and its prince—the devil—is judged. Our Lord promises to come again, always "soon." All the signs necessary for Him to return "on the clouds of heaven with power and great glory" (Matthew 24:30) are fulfilled. "Amen. Come, Lord Jesus!" (Revelation 22:20). At the same time, she prays for patience on the Lord's behalf, to do the work that is to be done "while it is day; night is coming, when no one can work" (John 9:4). That night falls on people already, all around and among us.

As we bear witness to the Holy Trinity in the world's last hours, we will face all manner of opposition from the "unholy trinity": the devil, who prowls and lies; the world, which seduces and distracts; and our sinful flesh, which wants what it wants and distrusts God unto death. Jesus has promised as much (John 15:18–16:15; Matthew 13:1–23), but He also promises that we will have His Word and Spirit and that these will not fail us. As Paul says, the Gospel "is the power of God for salvation to everyone who believes" (Romans 1:16), and "in all these things we are more than conquerors through Him who loved us" (8:37). Each challenge the devil, the world, and the sinful flesh present is at the same time an opportunity for us to speak the Word of God with confidence in its power, confessing before others that our Lord Jesus has overcome the world (Matthew 10:16–33; John 16:33) and looking forward to the day when He will also claim us before our Father in heaven.

Suffering and Death

Leaving aside the dreaded "isms" for a moment, let's talk about something common and just as troubling: suffering and death. At these, people of whatever belief tend to cry out, "Why?" One's natural inclination is to (a) try to answer, any answer, as quickly as possible to fill the awkward silence or even more awkward sobbing and (b) get home and think, "Rats! I really wish I'd said . . ." I often wonder why God keeps cutting with such a dull knife as myself, but that doesn't mean I should bury myself in the junk drawer and hope He finds someone else to cut with! It's worth getting sharpened up a bit before He puts us in a place and gives us the chance to speak.

The world hastens to answer the question, "Why?" because it feels some security in having an explanation. Jesus' own disciples, when they came upon a man born blind, asked, " 'Who sinned, this man or his parents, that he was born blind?' Jesus answered, 'It was not that this man sinned, or his parents, but that the works of God might be displayed in him' " (John 9:2–3). The answer isn't in an explanation—and that should be a relief, for we're not good at right answers. Look how Job's friends and even his wife tried to explain his woes and find a way out of them and only made Job's suffering worse. Better friends know the answer is not in figuring out why, how, who's to blame, and who isn't. The answer is in Jesus, and you know this Jesus and can talk about Him.

The minor details of God's plan for us and for the world are and will remain a mystery to us (though they are not so to God). But we have His promise that "all things work together for good, for those who are called according to His purpose" (Romans 8:28), and we know what that purpose is. The whole creation, Paul says just before that, "was subjected to futility, not of itself, but because of Him who subjected it, in hope" (Romans 8:20, author's translation). In that hope, we groan— creation groans—even the Spirit groans within us when we can't find the words. This lasts a time, but that hope will not fail, the hope of salvation in Christ Jesus, the firstfruits from the dead.

Like the bite of the fiery serpents in the wilderness (Numbers 21:4–9), our sufferings and trials in this life are ultimately for one purpose only: to turn our eyes to the One lifted up for us, so that clinging firmly to God's promise and assured of Jesus' death and resurrection, we may live (John 3:9–17). "For God so loved the world, that He gave His only Son." The oft-asked question is "How can a loving God . . . ?" The answer is Jesus, only Jesus. God has lifted Him up from the earth so that all who look on and believe in Him should be saved and that He should draw all men to Himself. The one thing that simply must be in our witness (if we are going to witness to Christ) is Jesus, crucified for sins, risen for justification, and victorious over death.

What do sins have to do with it? We ought not connect the dots quite so quickly as the disciples tried to. "He did thus and such, so, boom, disaster!" God has not told us that. Reason might favor a simple cause-and-effect explanation, but the story is almost always more complicated. We are not there to play pathologist but to proclaim Jesus. Generally, grieving brings with it much guilt. The death of a loved one or some other loss brings a flood of regret over what could or should have been. Assurance of forgiveness and new life in Christ, even for the yet-living, is never out of place and may be just the right word at the right time, spoken ever so gently and with all due respect.

This sort of comfort far surpasses the generic God-talk we often hear. And it should! Take time to listen. Silence doesn't have to be awkward. Don't assume you know the immediate answers before you know the immediate questions, worries, and fears. Moving with gentleness and respect, you can try to help get on to the ultimate answer, for " 'the word is near you, in your mouth and in your heart' (that is, the word of faith that we proclaim)" (Romans 10:8).

When you write a message of comfort, console a grieving friend, or try to restore hope to the downtrodden, delve into what you have been taught: the comforting and familiar words of the liturgy, of particular psalms, of hymn stanzas full of Jesus and His promises, of the Gospels and Epistles, and even of the catechism. You are not as short on material as you often think you are. You can't raise the dead or make up stories to comfort people. Sometimes we wish we could, but that's not a faithful witness. Rather, show them Jesus, the real Jesus, who enters into our suffering to give us life. The Word of God is near you, and its comfort is abundant. Put some time and thought into crafting an accurate, faithful, and helpful witness.

Disappointment with the Church and with Christians

Christ never says, "The Church would be a great place, except for the sinners." The Church is for sinners, for the forgiveness of sins. Yet we are often shocked and dismayed to find that the Church is full of them. (Well, full of us, to be perfectly honest—for who isn't one?) You will likely find folks who say, when asked why they have separated themselves from the Church or why they aren't interested in what the Church has to say, in effect, "The Church is full of hypocrites." "How could Christians treat me the way they did?" "They never accepted me there." "On Christmas Eve in 1978,

Edith Buddinsky glared at my toddler and made him cry, and I never went back." Okay, I made that last one up, but I've heard close to it.

Facts are one thing and statistics are another, but we all know people who have rotated in and out of churches or just wandered off. They're a tough crowd for our witness. The author of Hebrews at first holds out slim hope for the return of those who have experienced the Gospel and then wandered away—"impossible," in fact. They have considered and discarded as useless the things that would restore them (6:4–8). Yet, "though we speak in this way, yet in your case, beloved, we feel sure of better things—things that belong to salvation" (v. 9). With God all things are possible. The Sower sows the seed even on well-trodden ground, and some takes root, because the seed is good (Matthew 13:1–23). So we pray the Lord to strengthen our faith and to send us to witness also to these.

A lot of these folks are dealing with accumulations of disappointment or hurt, some legitimate, some overblown or even made up as an excuse to stay away. It's hard to sort out, and tender feelings often surround these things. What is for sure is that they belong in the Church, not out on their own. A Christian witness does not have to be the Truth and Reconciliation Commission. You don't have to sort all that out, or even get into it all.

What you can do is get to the essence of what the Church is and is there for. Kindly and gently ask whom their staying away hurts. Remind them of who is there for them, regardless of who else happens to be in the pews. Remind them also what that Lord has for them, despite what hypocrites might be around or even despite what hypocrites each of us might by nature be. We might look at the Church and consider it a great place except for the sinners. Christ does not see it this way but welcomes us in—not to justify our sins, mind you— but He would justify us, all of us, by His blood. And there is plenty of that to go around.

Atheism/Materialism (and a Note on the Word of God)

The idea that the world and humans came into existence of themselves, by chance, and that there thus is no God is fashionable. But it's not as common as you might think, held by a small minority. A little more common, perhaps, is the idea that God created the world not quickly and specifically as the Bible says, but by some kind of convoluted evolutionary process. Some Christians argue that we should accept such an explanation so we don't have to convince our neighbors of a six-day creation on top of everything else. That is tempting, because for some people evolution is deeply ingrained in their worldview. However, this sort of compromise solution doesn't work because that's simply not the witness of the Bible, and the Bible is God's reliable Word.

What the Bible teaches about creation is important. God creates through His Word, the same Word we claim is full of power to forgive sins and create faith. Think of that! The existence of the whole world, which the Bible says is called forth out of nothing by His Word (Hebrews 11:3), is proof of what His Word can do also in us. Likewise, as God tells it, death is not there from the beginning. He did not make man to die. It is not part of a "circle of life." That's Disney, not the Bible. He made man to live (by faith, we might add). Death is "the wages of sin" (Romans 6:23). That is not really true if death is an integral part of the evolutionary mechanism by which man came to be. To be consistent, wrecking the first part of Romans 6:23—by denying the biblical fact that death is not natural but something God subjects the world to on account of sin (8:20–21)—would wreck the second part also, that "the free gift of God is eternal life in Christ Jesus our Lord." If we junk the first Adam, we junk the second (5:12–21).

Part of our fallenness is to have a "debased mind" and be "futile in [our] thinking," to deny the Creator in His creation (Romans 1). It should not surprise us that those who want to deny that God exists are able to interpret the evidence so. God does not give Himself to be fully known in rocks and fossils and radioactive decay and the light of the stars. He gives Himself to be fully

A good resource for exploring more about the relationship between science and Scripture is *5 Things You Can Do to Appreciate Science and Love the Bible*, a book in the You Can Do It! series.

known in Jesus, and Jesus and His apostles affirm the Genesis creation. There are many good and helpful resources out there that show how the physical evidence better supports the Bible's account of creation than it does the evolutionary theory, or even "old Earth" creationism. That may be your cup of tea, or it may not. But the best place to start with an atheist is with the simple facts about Jesus, the man who was also God, who died and rose again from the dead. That gets right to the point, doesn't it? In that is the seed that can burst into everything else. If Jesus rose from the dead—and the evidence surely is that He did!—then much of their worldview needs reevaluation, including, for an evolutionist, what death means and how the world came to be.

The Word of God, particularly the Gospel, is the power of God to save. The devil must attack the Word—and not only in Genesis 1–3, which is already embarrassing for the devil. This is his last chance, not to win, of course, but at least to take as many of Christ's already-purchased people with him as he can, before the Word brings about faith in them. He snatches up the seed (Matthew 13:1–23) as quickly as he can, for he knows, as Luther says, that "one little word can fell him" (*LSB* 656:3). There is a whole field of biblical apologetics that, like these books on creation, shows that—against centuries of biased reporting—the evidence supports the Bible as being everything it claims to be. Your pastor may be able to provide you some pointers in this area if you are interested.

A great, easy-to-read resource on the "science" of evolution is *In the Beginning, God,* by Joel Heck, available from CPH.

Postmodernism/Relativism

The creation-evolution debate is a factual argument. Both can't be true; it can't be just a matter of perception. Yet that's the kind of response we often get when trying to make a factual argument, especially from younger people: "That might be your truth, but my truth is this." We know that makes no sense—truth is truth, and only God is its Master, its Lord. But you've heard such as that, and now we give it a fancy name: postmodernism. Postmodern thought posits that everything is relative: there are truths, not "Truth," and each truth may be as good as any other—as long as your truth doesn't step on mine! Well, it's nothing new, just futile thinking (Romans 1:21) dressed up under a fancy name. Pilate asks, rhetorically, it seems, "What is truth?" (John 18:38). It has always been part of fallen human nature to imagine that we can call the shots, that what we say can dictate reality. That is the original sin, isn't it? "You will be like God," the serpent said (Genesis 3:5), able to say what's good and evil and make it so. That belief infects not just postmodernists but each of us, from Adam on.

Even folks who admit there's a God above them are usually awfully quick to assume that they can define Him more or less as they please or as they have interpreted their various experiences and feelings. Talk about who the true God is and you will get plenty of home-brew ideas offered in exchange. Often what they say is as ridiculous as the various judgments of the poet Saxe's blind men assessing the elephant: a wall, a snake, a spear, and so on. It can be a real trial to do as both Paul and Peter suggest and respond with gentleness and respect and yet with the truth, which is Jesus Himself as He really is, as He reveals Himself in Scripture, and not as anyone imagines Him.

Our witness to the real Christ who redeems us through real facts in the pivot point of the one history of the entire universe (Colossians 1:13–28) has to confront the postmodern idea that there is no one history, no one truth, that there can be no one story that binds everything together. For minds thoroughly ruined by postmodernism, this can be a tough nut to crack! Helpful, though, is Luther's insight that a god is meant to be trusted, that "whatever you set your heart on and put your trust in is truly your god" (Large Catechism I 3; see 1–3).

There is no point in a god that can't be trusted. A god who is only a psychological crutch or imaginary friend should be cast off as ultimately useless, just a reflection of the self and of one's own desires, hopes, and fears, a personification of the karmic rules supposed by humans to be those by which the world is run. Such a god cannot be trusted, for its will for us is never fully known, and it makes no promises. Such a god really isn't even a god, let alone the one true God. To have a god is to trust.

To be a faithful witness to a person whose denial of the one true God is grounded in a postmodern fantasy, one might aim to contrast the untrustworthiness of such an imaginary god and the worldview that props it up with the trustworthiness of the true God. The true God reveals Himself definitely in the flesh of Jesus and by definite means of Word and Sacrament, so that He can be known and trusted. In Luther's day, what we now recognize as postmodernism he would have classed under enthusiasm, meaning defining God within, out of our own spiritual hankerings and potential. But the true God speaks to us from outside, by means of His definite, prophetic, and apostolic Word (Smalcald Articles III VIII 3–13). This is not a burden but a great gift. The true God does not leave us to figure out who He is up there; rather, He entered in the flesh of Jesus into our world so we would not have to guess, so we could see the Son and have the Father (John 14:5–24).

Antinomianism/Libertinism

Americans like to be free, not to be told what to do. Perhaps our favorite verse in the Bible is "Judge not, that you be not judged" (Matthew 7:1), which we take out of all context to justify whatever we want to do. "Who are you to tell me that what I want and love and feel in my heart is wrong?" You've heard that or maybe have had that very passage hurled back at you.

The fact is, though, that the one living in sin is not free. Another way to put it is that the "freedom to sin" is only illusory. The devil pretends to be a gracious lord and master, more gracious, in fact, than the Lord, the only one who is good. Satan doesn't care how you live or what you do—to him, you might as well take as many people out with you as you can—so long as you do not repent and believe the Gospel. That is the only intolerance in his platform of tolerance because that is the only thing that will snatch you from his vindictive claws.

His platform is pretty well reflected in our present society. There is tolerance for everything but for the absolutes of Law and Gospel, to which we simply must bear witness. (Who knows what a faithful witness like that might cost us or the Church in coming days? Look at what it cost Jesus' first witnesses. But we have His good promises too [Matthew 5:11–12]). Even some Christians go with the flow. The devil is a wily foe. He will use a "gospel," perhaps that Jesus died to free you *to* sin, to replace the Gospel that Jesus died to free you *from* your sins, which is quite different. His version sounds a lot more appealing, but it is also infinitely less saving. He doesn't care if you use the word *Jesus*, as long as your trust is in anything except Jesus for the remission of sins.

Therefore, when you come bearing witness to the Law and wrath of God and to the only hope in the Gospel of Jesus, you will likely get the same reaction Jesus got when He said His Word would set men free: "We have not been slaves!" But Jesus tells the truth: "Everyone who practices sin is a slave to sin" (John 8:34; see also vv. 31–36).

Only the Spirit of God, working in and through the Word of God, can break these chains. The Holy Spirit must break a will opposed to God and establish faith. Preparing for that assault, He can use the hammer of God's wrath now being revealed in this world against all manner of ungodliness (Romans 1:18) to smash the façade of freedom the devil erects around sin. We can help gently, with respect, out of care and not vindictiveness, to point out the sort of bondage our sins have us in. They do not make us happy or our lives better. This is true not only of homosexuality and adultery and murder, but also of gossip, slander, disobedience, and ruthlessness. That our sins make us happy and free is a lie we easily believe, but on any real reflection, it is seen not to be true. We suffer in our own flesh the consequences of our rebellion (Romans 1:27), and ultimately that is why people are subjected to death. Yet, even in this, we have hope of repentance and faith.

As we said in the second chapter, this is our place for witness in humility, as fellow sinners, to the redemption—to the true freedom from sin and guilt, devil and death—that is in Christ Jesus and His glorious Means of Grace. The denial of God's Law leads to a denial of the Gospel, and that's a huge problem for our witness. But the power of God for salvation remains in the Gospel (Romans 1:16), and with Him all things are possible. So they are for us too, through Him who gives us strength.

Key Points

● We have Christ's promises that even when we speak against opposition or under persecution, He will be with and sustain us.

- A Christian witness should not enter into speculation but should listen and then patiently and diligently move to the ultimate answer, which is that God loves the world in this way: He gives His only Son.

- A Christian witness has to understand that some bad impressions may have to be unlearned before new ones can be made.

- The best Christian witness starts with Jesus, who is raised from the dead.

- Postmodernism claims that there is no truth, but we have *the* truth to proclaim.

- A Christian witness can gently point out the power of sin's bondage and that true freedom is found in repentance and the forgiveness of sins in Christ Jesus.

Discussion Questions

1. Perhaps, without revealing confidences, you can remember a situation where you dealt with one of the challenges addressed in this chapter. (If not, you can imagine one.) Discuss how you tried to clear the way for a clear Christian witness or how one might.

2. We previously noted that we, of ourselves, are no different from those we are witnessing to. We are sinners. It is Christ who has made us saints. We swim in a sea of these "isms" and many others, and we are not unaffected by them—we just don't usually slap those labels on

ourselves! Can you identify where these views, which threaten our faith, have tried to influence you or maybe have made inroads? How have you learned to detect them? Have you found ways to counter them?

3. What other obstacles have you found to your Christian witness? Where have you found the strength and wisdom to deal with them? Which ones stump you? Discuss as a group—and perhaps ask your pastor to address some of the most common ones!

Action Items

1. **Become at least an amateur apologist:** An apologist is one who defends the faith against worldly challenges or, perhaps better said, who studies how to break down worldly arguments against the Christian witness. Thinking on the people with whom you are often in contact, identify the most prominent obstacle to witness that you might encounter. Perhaps it might be one from this chapter, one I didn't have space to address, or maybe one I didn't even think of. With your pastor's help, find a book or two, or some other resource on the topic, and study up. Perhaps it will help you prepare to break down a wall that's keeping your neighbor from seeing the Gospel for what it is!

2. **Put on an apologetics event at your congregation:** Work with your pastor to identify a topic of apologetic interest, such as evidence of creation, history of the

Bible, chinks in the postmodernist's "truth armor," or reaching out to those hurt by the Church. Either encourage him to present on that topic (be nice, give him time and resources) or see if there would be interest in bringing in an expert to prepare your congregation's members to add apologetic tools to their witness.

3. **Be intentionally reflective on your Christian witness.** (This one probably applies to the whole book, in hope that it will be of some lasting value.) When you notice a chance to act or speak in witness, don't let it slip by unexamined. Make time later to think about what you said and what the hearers seem to have heard, what they said or didn't say in reply. Think about what obstacles may have gotten in the way, what "errors in transmission" might have occurred, or what opportunities you only saw in hindsight. If you like to journal, you could even jot down a few thoughts. Take stock from time to time. Maybe visit with your pastor if you see things you'd like to brush up on or get reactions you just don't understand. Witness is an organic part of your Christian life, but that doesn't mean you can't reflect on it, pray for it, and work toward growing in it. May the Holy Spirit richly bless you and those around you as you do.

If in reading this book you'd hoped for a script or formula for witnessing, this certainly was not it. Lutheran pastors are often asked for easy answers when the real answer is living by faith. That simply has to be lived out under God's grace as He works all things for good in the holy mystery of Christ. One script does not fit all.

As I was writing, some dear and faithful friends told me of a visit made to them years ago based on one of those other books. Some pious visitors sat awkwardly in their living room and asked the then inactive husband and father the script's ultimate serious question of the day: "If you were to die tonight, would you go to heaven?" I'm not sure any script could have prepared them for where to go next from his immediate and heartfelt answer: "I sure as hell hope so!"

So please don't be too disappointed that I haven't given you a script. Knowing your catechism, your Lord, and His service and having a real relationship forged in love for those to whom you speak—I think these prepare you better than any script could. This is only a beginning; as I've said before, witness is an organic part of the Christian life you already live, a journey you're probably already on. But I hope it has you headed more confidently in that good direction. I am glad if, even in some small way, this little book has helped better to prepare you, as Peter says, "to make a defense to anyone who asks you for a reason for the hope that is in you" (1 Peter 3:15).